PICASSO:
MY GRANDFATHER

Marina Picasso is the founder of several charitable organisations that help underprivileged children in Vietnam. She has five children, including three adopted Vietnamese children, and lives in La Californie, the villa in the South of France that she inherited from Picasso.

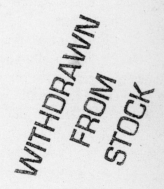

Marina Picasso

PICASSO: MY GRANDFATHER

TRANSLATED BY
Catherine Temerson

VINTAGE

Published by Vintage 2002

2 4 6 8 10 9 7 5 3 1

Copyright © Editions Denoël 2001
Written with the collaboration of Louis Valentin
English translation © Catherine Temerson 2001

Vincent O'Sullivan's translation of Baudelaire is taken from
Baudelaire in English, ed. Carol Clark & Robert Sykes
(Penguin Books, 1997)

First published in Great Britain by
Chatto & Windus 2001

Vintage
Random House, 20 Vauxhall Bridge Road,
London SW1V 2SA

Random House Australia (Pty) Limited
20 Alfred Street, Milsons Point, Sydney
New South Wales 2061, Australia

Random House New Zealand Limited
18 Poland Road, Glenfield,
Auckland 10, New Zealand

Random House (Pty) Limited
Endulini, 5A Jubilee Road, Parktown 2193,
South Africa

The Random House Group Limited Reg. No. 954009
www.randomhouse.co.uk

A CIP catalogue record for this book
is available from the British Library

ISBN 0 099 43703 1

Printed and bound in Great Britain by
Cox & Wyman Limited, Reading, Berkshire

To my children, with all my heart,
in alphabetical order

Dimitri
Flore
Florial
Gaël
May

Contents

'To make a dove, you must first wring its neck.'
PICASSO

— 1 —

There's no running away from Picasso. I know that. I have never succeeded. But when I had my breakdown, I still hadn't realized this.

It must have been one o'clock in the afternoon. I was in Geneva, driving down the Quai Gustave-Ador in a steady flow of traffic, taking my children, Gaël and Flore, to school. On my right was the lake Geneva and its famous *Jet d'Eau*.

The lake . . . the cars . . . the *Jet d'Eau* . . . and, suddenly, I was in the grip of a violent panic attack. My fingers contracted in an unbearable cramp. I felt a burning spasm in my chest. My heart was pounding. I was suffocating. I was going to die. I had just enough time to tell the children to stay calm before I collapsed with my head on the wheel. Paralysed. Was I going mad?

I had stopped the car right in the middle of the road. Other cars sped by, almost grazing mine, honking at me to move on. No one stopped . . .

After half an hour of anguish, I managed to re-start the car, park it on the kerb and drag myself over to the petrol station a few yards away. I had to call for help. I didn't want to be put away. What would happen to my children?

'You need therapy,' the doctor said.

Things were so bad I had nothing to lose.

So began my analysis. It would last fourteen years. Fourteen years of uncontrollable tears, fainting fits and screams. I writhed in pain as I inched my way back in time to relive the things that had destroyed me — silent, then stammering — finally to express what had been buried deep within the little girl and then the adolescent . . . and had eaten her alive.

Fourteen years of misery to rectify so many years of unhappiness.

Because of Picasso.

Picasso's quest for the absolute entailed an implacable will to power. His extraordinary work demanded human sacrifices. He engulfed anyone who got near him, and drove them to despair.

No one in my family managed to escape his stranglehold. He needed blood to sign each of his paintings: my father's blood, my brother's, my mother's, my grandmother's, and mine; the blood of all those who loved him — people who thought that they loved a human being, whereas instead they loved Picasso.

My father was born under the yoke of his tyranny; he died from it — betrayed, disappointed, demeaned. Destroyed.

My brother Pablito, the plaything of Picasso's sadism and indifference, committed suicide at twenty-four by drinking a lethal dose of bleach. I found him lying in his own blood, his oesophagus and larynx burned, his stomach wrecked, his heart adrift. I held his hand for three months at La Fontonne Hospital in Antibes as he lay slowly dying. With this horrendous act he had wanted put an end to his suffering and to bypass the problems awaiting him. Problems that awaited me too, for we were the stillborn descendants of Picasso, trapped in a spiral of mocked hopes.

My grandmother Olga, humiliated and degraded by so much betrayal, ended her life paralysed. Not once did my grandfather come to see her when she was bedridden and in distress. Yet she had given up everything for him – her country, her career, her dreams and her pride.

As for my mother, she wore the name Picasso like a badge, a badge that lifted her to the highest rungs of paranoia. In marrying my father she had married Pablo Picasso. In her delirium, she could not accept the fact that the great man didn't want to see her or give her the 'grand' life she deserved. Fragile, lost and unstable, she had to make do with part of the meagre weekly allowance which my grandfather paid to keep his son and grandchildren under his domination – and on the verge of poverty.

I wish that I could live without this past.

It's a Thursday in November. My father is leading me by the hand. Silently, he walks up to the forbidding gate which protects La Californie, my grandfather's house. My brother Pablito follows, hands clasped behind his back. I am six, Pablito nearly eight.

My father rings the bell. I am afraid, as I always am each time we come. There is the sound of footsteps, then a key turning in the lock and La Californie's concierge, an elderly Italian worn by servitude, appears behind the half-open gate. He looks us over and says to my father, 'Do you have an appointment, Monsieur Paul?'

'Yes,' my father stammers.

He has let go of my hand so I won't feel how moist his palm is.

'Good,' the elderly concierge replies, 'I'll see if the Maître can receive you.'

The gate closes behind him. It's raining. In the air is the scent of the eucalyptus trees which, with their peeling bark, line the path where we are left to wait for the Maître's orders.

Just like last Saturday, or the Thursday before that.

In the distance a dog is barking. Lump, my grandfather's dachshund. He likes me and lets me stroke him.

The wait is endless. Pablito is now clinging to me, both to comfort me and to feel less lonely himself. My father has finished his cigarette. He puts it out and lights another. His fingers are stained with nicotine.

'You'd better wait in the car,' he whispers as though afraid that someone might hear him.

'No,' we answer in chorus. 'We're staying with you.'

Our hair is matted from the rain. We feel guilty.

Once again the key turns in the gate and the wrinkled Italian appears. He lowers his eyes. In a discouraged voice, he recites the lesson he has memorized: 'The Maître can't see you today. Madame Jacqueline has asked me to tell you that he's working.'

Even he's not fooled. He's ashamed.

How many Thursdays had we heard those words – 'the Maître is working,' 'the Maître is sleeping,' 'the Maître is not here' – at the locked gate of La Californie, which was defended like a fortress. Occasionally it was Jacqueline Roque, the future, devoted Madame Picasso, who delivered the sentence: 'The Sun does not want to be disturbed.'

When it wasn't the Sun, it was Monseigneur or the Grand Maître. We didn't dare show our feelings of disappointment and humiliation in front of her.

On the days when the gate was opened for us, we would follow my father across the gravelled courtyard up to the entrance of the house. I used to count the paces like the beads of a rosary. It came to exactly sixty hesitant, guilty steps.

Inside the Titan's den – Ali Baba's treasure cave – clutter reigned supreme. A mass of paintings rested on paint-splattered easels, sculptures lay everywhere, crates overflowed with African masks. There were cardboard boxes, old newspapers, stretchers for unpainted canvases, tin cans, ceramic tiles, armchair feet bristling with upholsterer's tacks, musical instruments, bicycle handlebars, profiles cut out of sheet metal and, on the wall, posters for bullfights, reams of drawings, portraits of Jacqueline, bulls' heads . . .

Amidst this shambles, where we are made to wait once again, we feel unwanted. My father helps himself to a glass of whisky and empties it in one – no doubt to give himself composure and courage. Pablito has sat down on a chair and pretends to play with a lead soldier that he's taken out of his pocket.

'Don't make noise and don't touch anything' says Jacqueline who has slipped into the room. 'The Sun will be down in a minute.'

Esméralda, my grandfather's goat, follows her. Esméralda can do anything she wants: gambol through the house, test her horns against the furniture, leave her droppings on the drawings and canvases piled in a jumble on the floor. Esméralda is at home. We are intruders.

We hear a flurry of laughter and shouts . . . My

grandfather makes his dramatic entrance, thundering and heroic.

I say grandfather, but we're not allowed to call him grandfather. It's forbidden. We're supposed to call him Pablo, like everyone else. Instead of abolishing frontiers, this 'Pablo' confines us to anonymity; it creates a boundary between the inaccessible demiurge and us.

'Hello, Pablo,' my father says as he goes up to him. 'Did you sleep well?'

He too must call him Pablo.

Pablito and I run up and throw our arms around him. We're children. We need a grandfather.

He pats us on the head, like you stroke the neck of a horse.

'So, Marina, tell me. Are you a good girl? And you, Pablito, how are you doing at school?'

Empty questions that don't need answers. A way of manipulating us into feeling close to him when it happens to suit him.

He takes us to the room where he paints: the studio he has chosen for a day, a week or a month, before creating another, as he moves wherever the house, his inspiration, or whim, take him. Here nothing is forbidden. We're allowed to touch the brushes, draw on his notebooks, cover ourselves in paint. It amuses him.

'I'll make you a surprise,' he says, laughing.

He rips a sheet of paper out of his notebook, folds it over several times incredibly fast and, magically, his powerful hands produce a little dog, a flower, a paper chicken.

'Do you like it?' he asks in his husky voice.

Pablito says nothing while I stammer, 'It's . . . beautiful!'

We would like to take them home with us, but we're

not allowed . . . They're the work of Picasso.

At the time I didn't realize that these figures made of paper, cardboard or matches, all these illusions he created like a conjurer, were part of an ambition that I now find monstrous: to make us understand subconsciously that he was all-powerful and we were nothing. All he had to do was scratch a sheet of paper with his nail, cut up a piece of cardboard with scissors, spread a splotch of paint on a fold. Out came violent, pagan images that crushed us. But I'm also convinced that he felt lonely and wanted to recapture childhood. Not ours, but his own, over there in Malaga when, with a single pencil stroke, he would bewitch his young cousins, Maria and Concha, by producing imaginary creatures out of the void. That was the kind of audience he enjoyed. Like Pablito and I: raw, as yet undamaged material that he could manipulate according to his mood. He had behaved like this towards his son from the start, with his paintings of Paulo on his donkey, Paulo holding a lamb, Paulo with the slice of bread, Paulo dressed as a *torero*, Paulo as Harlequin . . . before turning him into the inadequate father of my childhood.

My father, present as he always is when we come to La Californie, doesn't dare interrupt these special moments with our grandfather. He walks furtively from the studio to the kitchen with a worried, feverish look in his eye. He pours himself another glass of whisky or returns from the kitchen with a glass of wine. He is drinking too much. In a short while he will have to confront my grandfather and ask him for money for us and my mother, money that Picasso owes him − the words pain me − for his loyal service. He is Picasso's chauffeur, paid by the week, his

7

factotum with no life of his own, a marionette whose strings Picasso enjoys tangling, his whipping boy.

'Say, Paulo, your children are no fun. They should relax.'

We are terrified of breaking the spell. We must make sure everything goes well. For my father, and my mother, who will ask later how everything went, we must play along and please Picasso.

He grabs a hat lying on a chair, snatches a cape off a peg and drapes it over his shoulders, jumping up and down like a puppet. He shouts and claps his hands extravagantly.

'Come on,' his eyes flash. 'Copy me. Cheer up and play.'

We clap our hands at his clowning. My father joins in, goading his father, a cigarette stuck in the corner of his mouth, his eyes watering from the smoke.

'*Anda*, Pablo! *Anda, anda!*'

An ovation shouted in Spanish, the language of the Picassos, the only link between the omnipotent father and the belittled son.

Galvanized, my grandfather picks up a wooden spoon and a teatowel from the table: his sword and *muleta*. With a bright, barbarous look in his eye, he performs a series of passes for us – *manolinetas, chicuelinas, verónicas, mariposas* – to the rhythm of my father's '*olé*'s, and mine.

Pablito is silent and looks away. His face is deathly pale. He suffers from not having a proper family, with a responsible father, a lenient mother, a loving grandfather. Pablito and I are not destined for such things.

The east wind has chased away the clouds and a timid sun sheds a holy light into the room. My father has still not dared broach the subject of money with my grandfather. Why annoy him? He's in such a good mood.

Today, I can easily imagine the torments he went through when he had to approach my grandfather. He had been so adulated and pampered as a child and now he had hardly any worth in Picasso's eyes. What had become of the Harlequin who had posed for his father wearing a yellow and blue chequered costume and a tulle ruff around his neck? Do the Picasso enthusiasts notice how sad Harlequin looks in the painting? How his expression begs for a bit of love? He already knew he would never be allowed to grow up.

At the age of ten, or twenty, my father might still have escaped from the curse. Then, he still had the energy to save his skin. If he didn't, it was because, subconsciously, he must have realized that in leaving Picasso he would be denying him a part of his work. Long before his father had clipped his wings, he could not leave. As an only son he was under an obligation not leave. He was a piece of the Picasso puzzle, just like each of the paintings. He was so intent on not breaking up this puzzle that, when his mother died and left him some of the paintings by Picasso she had owned, he declined to accept them so as not to deprive Picasso, his god.

Whatever this god said was the gospel truth, including all the humiliating words and insults. Once, in my presence, Picasso said to my father, 'It's ridiculous to use a nail file. Do what I do, file them against the corner of a wall.' I saw my father do this when I was little. It made me sick with shame. I also saw him push away his fork and eat his fish with his hands because that was what his father did.

To model oneself on Picasso was an honour.

Grandfather has opened the bay window looking out on the garden where two miniature goats are cavorting around the tall, wet grass. Esméralda is chained to the tail of her bronze counterpart; she is dodging the attacks of Lump, the dachshund, who is trying to nibble her legs. Yan, the old boxer, who is gradually losing his eyesight, crawls up to Pablito and licks his hand.

I'm filled with sudden joy and feel gloriously light-hearted. For the first time since our arrival, Pablito and I are free to be real children.

That garden at La Californie, with Pablito holding my hand, is my loveliest memory of my visits to Picasso. In summer, the rosemary bushes mixed their scent with the broom, bindweed besieged the flowering mimosa branches, and clusters of poppies, buttercups and wallflowers shot up everywhere. Wherever you looked, there was a jumble of wild grass and fragrant plants set off by palm, pine, cypress and eucalyptus trees beautifully silhouetted against the blue Mediterranean sky. Nestling in the midst of this deliberately neglected stretch of land was a population of plaster, clay and bronze sculptures: a female monkey, a skull, a pregnant woman, a bust of Marie-Thérèse Walter, a cat, an owl. There were ceramics and pottery, some covered with velvety patches of moss, others fresh out of the kiln.

I also remember the parrot on its perch, the butterflies fluttering from flower to flower, and the pigeons, turtle-doves and doves flying to their aviary under the roof whenever we mischievously tried to catch them.

In the spring, we knew exactly where the violets hid. It was a secret corner of paradise that was ours alone.

It's time to leave. Grandfather is sitting at the table and we're standing next to him. In front of him are the remains of a light meal, eaten in haste while we were playing outside. We peer at a basket of dried fruit. We haven't eaten and are famished. Grandfather notices our gaze. Smiling, he picks out a date and a fig from the basket and slices them in half with his pocket knife. He breaks open a walnut, shells it and stuffs it into the date and fig, squeezing the two together with his fingers.

'Come here,' he says, still smiling.

We approach shyly, eyes half-closed, and open our mouths wide. Gently, almost religiously, grandfather drops the sweetmeat into our mouths.

It is a kind of sacrament.

Scanning my memories as far back as I can, the only mark of love I can remember ever receiving from him was this stuffed fig and date. The only gift of himself that he ever bestowed on us.

My father has finally succeeded in speaking to his father – they hold a long secret conversation at the far end of the studio. This is a private discussion between a six-foot-two, weak colossus and a five-foot-three, all-powerful dwarf. My grandfather digs into his pocket and takes out a wad of notes, which my father seizes furtively.

'Thank you, Pablo.'

The perfidious response is immediate: 'You're incapable of supporting your children. You're incapable of making a living. You're incapable of doing anything. You're second-rate and will always be second-rate. You're a waste of my time.'

In short, 'I am *El Rey*, the King, and you are my object.'

An object that he had slowly, methodically, wrecked so that it wouldn't trouble him.

Later, much later, I would learn that the figs and dates stuffed with nuts that grandfather gave us each time we came for a visit were called *mendiants* – beggars.

There are things we would be better off not knowing.

2

'Paul Picasso, do you take Emilienne Lotte as your lawful wedded wife . . .'

One fateful day, my mother and father stood in front of the mayor and expressed the wish to be joined together for life. With a mutual 'I do' they swore reciprocal love and fidelity and pledged to love, protect and support their children. Unfortunately Pablito and I were not in luck. Paul Picasso and Emilienne Lotte, who took such pride in becoming Madame Picasso, separated when I was six months old and my brother almost two. This break-up was inevitable. Neither my mother nor my father had a talent for happiness.

Sitting in the back of the Oldsmobile – the car my grandfather gave to my father so he can chauffeur him around – we leave La Californie and Cannes and drive to Golfe-Juan where my mother is waiting.

Staring into the rear-view mirror, I see the look in my father's eyes – an empty, desperate look. I never saw him laugh or just be happy. When things went well at La Californie, he sometimes joked or appeared to enjoy himself, but it wasn't natural to him. He did it to please Picasso, to conform to his desire, become that desire. His own desires were nonexistent. He had swept them aside once and for all and gradually allowed himself to be absorbed by the god – and yet he couldn't identify with him entirely. The image he had before him was that of a monstrous father who destroyed, mistreated, disdained, scorned and humiliated. An insolent father who only had to sign a paper tablecloth in a restaurant to pay the bill for forty people, who boasted of being able to buy a house without needing a lawyer by handing over three paintings that he haughtily described as 'three pieces of crap smeared in the night'.

My father could not create his own identity through such images.

For a long time he had dreamed of becoming a motorcycle racing driver. He was intoxicated by the speed and the noise, the wind in his hair, the forty-five-degree curves, and the danger. His Norton Manx was his pride and joy. It obeyed him like an extension of his own body, responding to the slightest pressure of the accelerator. With it, he could challenge his father's sovereignty, free himself, and finally become a Picasso.

But it is impossible to imagine two Picassos in the same family; that would be treason.

My grandfather said no. 'I command you to give up this stupidity. That's an order. I don't want you to kill yourself. Speed frightens me.' And once again: 'I don't want to hear any more about it. You're a bourgeois anarchist as well as an incompetent.'

In her book *Life with Picasso*, Françoise Gilot gives a succinct description of the rebelliousness that welled up in my father when Picasso scorned him this way. She describes how, tired of hearing his father say he was a good for nothing, Paulo announced that at least he was good at riding a motorcycle. He took part in a race that left from Monte-Carlo and zigzagged along the cliff roads beside the Mediterranean, and came in second among professionals. This was probably one of the only times that my father stood up to Picasso and showed him that life did not necessarily revolve around him – one of the only times that he let him know he had his own dreams and his own life.

My father could never find the opening that might have allowed him to become a man. As a young boy, his future was already sealed.

My grandfather, as a way of opposing my grandmother Olga, to whom he was no longer attracted, vengefully set her own son against her. At first this was done with small brushstrokes – discreet and Machiavellian. For example, when Paulo was six and trying hard to be well behaved at the table, watched attentively by his mother, Picasso would walk in, grinning, and slip a small toy car into his hand. My father, who got the message, would look defiantly at his mother and start rolling the car around in his bowl of soup. What did a mother's disillusionment matter, or the fact that she wanted to give her only son a good upbringing? The only thing that mattered was the pleasure the father felt at setting his child against the wife he hated – and that my father would certainly have loved if Picasso hadn't spent his time slandering her.

The only lessons Paulo learned from his father were these: 'There's no point in being good at school. It serves no purpose. At San Rafael, the school in Malaga where my parents put me out of desperation, I was hopeless at everything. That hasn't prevented me from succeeding.'

14

Or: 'Keep trying to do something – but I know it won't amount to anything.'

I don't want to speak ill of Picasso. I just want to try and explain my long uphill struggle to rehabilitate the image of a man who was incapable of love. I'd like to make our suffering palpable. The Picasso virus to which we fell victim was subtle and undetectable. It was a combination of promises not kept, abuse of power, mortification, contempt and, above all, incommunicability. It paralysed my father's will, warped my mother's judgement, destroyed my grandmother's health and – in spite of the fact that children overflow with energy – made my brother and me regress to the state of foetuses. We were defenceless against it. There was no antidote. Invariably and relentlessly, our vaguest, tiniest desires were met with the terrible sentence: 'Whatever you attempt, you will not survive.'

It was not necessarily Picasso who passed this judgement. It was also all the people who granted my grandfather power, who glorified him, venerated him, and raised him to the level of God: the experts, art historians, curators, critics, not to mention courtiers, parasites, bootlickers who were so impressed by what my grandfather could do so effortlessly that they fantasized about him. They didn't care whether my grandfather was happy or unhappy, the only thing that mattered was his power, his empire, and the wealth he represented. To them he was a showman.

For a long time, without knowing why, I had a great tenderness for tramps. I used to picture my grandfather as a tramp under a bridge in Paris, the city he loved. I imagined him in his old sleeping bag, dirty and destitute, but so rich in his heart and so touching. I talked to him about everything and nothing; I explained that I was his granddaughter and just wanted to love him.

For as long as I live, I will always regret never having been able to talk to my grandfather in the way I wanted to. I wish the monstrous grandfather that I knew were still alive like his painting. With time I would have taught him how to become a loving grandfather like the kind man under the Paris bridge who knew how to listen to me and let me get close to him.

Yet another reason to grieve.

The Route Nationale 7. Below is the railway where the train glides by with its blue-tinted windows; on the left the Pont de l'Aube leading to the beach; in the distance the lighthouse of La Garoupe. At this time of day, its beacon is still faint . . . Pablito guilty takes my hand and holds it. In five minutes, we'll be with our mother. We so want everything to be all right. My father parks the Oldsmobile on the kerb of the avenue that runs along the seafront. He gets out, but before letting us out of the back seat, he religiously wipes some dust off the windshield. It is the reflex of a well-trained chauffeur. He walks slowly across the road, leading Pablito and me by the hand, and we plunge into the Rue Chabrier.

This is where we live – on the second floor of a modest building.

Outside Madame Alzeari, our ground-floor neighbour, is emptying her rubbish. 'So, children,' she clucks, 'Did you have a nice day? How's your grandfather?'

She wipes her hands on the front of her apron and addresses my father.

'Monsieur Paul, you don't look well. You should look after yourself.'

She strokes our heads and adds, 'These are very nice children you have.'

We like Madame Alzeari. She gives us sweets when we visit her.

We rush up the stairs, leaving our father behind. We're happy to be home. My mother has heard our footsteps. She's standing on the landing, wearing a tight sweater and a black leatherette miniskirt.

'I suppose once again, you haven't eaten,' she says. 'Go into the kitchen. You'll find some leftovers.'

We dash inside without even saying goodbye. In the kitchen we find some unfinished pasta and half an apple. My mother receives our father in the hall and takes the money. We are glad we aren't present for their conversation, which will turn sour, as usual. My mother has already started.

'What! That's all he gave you? How can you expect me to survive on this with two children? Your Picasso couldn't care less if I can't pay the gas and electricity bills. He doesn't give a damn if his grandchildren don't have enough to eat. Did you tell him that Marina needs a winter coat? That your son needs a pair of shoes? Did you tell him how we live? Did you tell him . . .'

An unchanging litany spouted in a high-pitched, hysterical voice, followed, of course, by the merciless blow below the belt: 'I know you. You'll use what you've pocketed to pay back your debts at the café and treat your mates to a round of drinks.'

My father's replies are unjust, extreme and brutal. 'What I do is none of your business. I can understand why Pablo hates you. You're stark raving mad.'

Shrieks, insults, violence . . .

In the kitchen, Pablito and I cling to each other at the

foot of the radiator and sob silently while munching our miserable apple.

We feel guilty.

Even though all this happened years ago, I still sometimes wake up in tears from nightmares which resurrect and magnify these sounds and images: the screams, my mother with her claws out, my father brutally pushing her away, Pablito and his tooth-marks on the apple. And, in the background, my grandfather's piercing eyes punishing me for still being alive.

Since he knew his son was helpless and that my mother had absolutely no means of support, why didn't Picasso tell his lawyers to pay a monthly allowance for his grand-children? Even the most modest of sums would have allowed my mother to manage her expenses, instead of constantly begging shop owners for credit.

But that would have been too simple, too human. Picasso, who was diabolical, knew full well what he was doing with this roundabout route: it served to make my father feel guilty and dependent and, in turn, make us dependent on his son. It was a hellish alchemy that made my father easier to crush and Picasso increasingly powerful.

The door has been slammed on my father and my mother is slumped in a chair, panting for breath. Her face is contorted and mascara is running down her cheeks. Suddenly she sits up and beckons us to come closer. Miraculously, she's smiling.

'So, how was it at your grandfather's?'

It's best not to answer. It's dangerous.

'That was a question,' she says, insistently.

'Fine,' Pablito mumbles. 'It went very well.'

'Did he talk about me?'

'A little bit,' Pablito answers. 'He asked how you were.'

'That's it.'

'Yes.'

The cross-examination is over. She knows that, unlike children who like to describe everything they've seen and done in the course of the day, we won't let her extract anything from us.

But she doesn't give up.

'Oh,' she starts in a heart-rending voice, 'that bastard has decided to push me away. With all his money, he thinks he can buy my silence, but that won't stop me from saying that he did everything he could to abuse me. You should have seen him when he was here in Golfe-Juan and he saw me walk past the terrace at the Hôtel de la Plage. He was always running after me, telling me I was beautiful. Oh, if I'd wanted . . .'

Sheer madness, a need to talk, to recount her life – a life that was her own fabrication.

Then, out of blue, she forgets about Picasso and tells us about meeting our father, how athletic he was and the charm he exuded. She describes the thrill she felt riding on his motorbike, arms wrapped around his waist, her senses awakened by the high speed and the exciting sensation of her body against his.

'I would have torn down mountains for him. I would have sacrificed my life . . .'

A theatrical sigh and then these hurtful words: 'Oh, there's no mistaking he's the son of his monstrous father!'

The monstrous father. If only she could finally expel her gall, take revenge, tear him to bits. 'If he thinks I'm impressed with his money and his name, he's wrong. I'm as strong as he is and I'll destroy him.'

A long silence and, without regard for us, she returns to her first meeting with Picasso, over-blowing his passion for her – a passion expressed by a telling, unmistakable stare.

'When it comes to men,' she says, 'I'm never wrong!'

To hear her talk, my grandfather resented her for not yielding to his advances. To hear her talk, he had chosen her for his son. It was an arranged marriage.

My mother always believed that being Picasso's daughter-in-law gave her a kind of divine right. She never worried about what would become of us later in life since a lucky star had made us Picassos like her. Picasso had become the predominant figure in her life. Everything revolved around him; he coloured all her thoughts. He was her only subject of conversation – with shopkeepers and with people she met in the street, even when she didn't know them.

'I'm Picasso's daughter-in-law.'

It was like a trophy, a special permit, an excuse for any eccentricity.

I can still remember how ashamed I felt in the summer, when she arrived on the beach in a silver or gold bikini, leaning on the arm of some Adonis fifteen years younger than her. And how humiliated I was as a young teenager when she would walk into a meeting of students and parents dressed in a miniskirt, with a young man barely older than I was. How I had to call her Mienne – short for Emilienne – because it sounded more youthful and more American. My fear when she started to talk, and how my heart sank when she explained Picasso's painting – she who had never seen so much as a catalogue or brochure of my grandfather's work.

Her way of talking varied according to whom she was

with. With people she hardly knew, she put Picasso on a pedestal: 'My father-in-law is a genius. I admire him and I know he likes me a lot.' With her more intimate acquaintances, she couldn't resist telling all: 'Can you imagine, with all his wealth, that bastard won't give us a penny.'

People laughed. People always laugh when things like this happen to others.

I don't remember my mother telling us stories like 'Little Red Riding Hood' or taking us for rides on a merry-go-round. And yet, however pathological she might have been, she was the only person to protect us. Apart from her, no one else in that family wanted us. In spite of her delusions of grandeur and her unruliness, she gave us the warmth of her presence, her motherly smell, her voice and her laughter, even if it was often forced. She made us a home in an apartment that had all the emotional features of early childhood memories: a whistling kettle, a kitchen table covered with oilcloth, a dripping tap, a wobbly chair that you were not supposed to sit on, a vase of dry flowers, and the cocoon-like blue bedroom where Pablito and I could isolate ourselves. These are incomparable treasures when you feel like an orphan.

As for the rest, she made do with what was given to her and did what she could – which wasn't much.

She might have been a perfectly dignified woman if she hadn't been infected by the Picasso virus. She was born into a bourgeois Protestant family from Lyons that included teachers, engineers and scientists. It was an academic, peaceful, no-nonsense family – in fact, too academic, too peaceful and too no-nonsense: she left it to marry a man who owned a pottery in Vallauris. With the fruits of their labour, they bought the apartment in Golfe-

Juan where they lived in discord, quarrelling and soon hating each other.

They divorced and, after a short breather, she met my father. My father whom she would marry . . . for better and especially for worse.

After separating from my father, my mother went with a lot of men, or I should say adolescents, whom she preferred because they made her feel more youthful. She picked them up on the beach in summer and in bars in winter, and she brought them home. They arrived with their long hair, flowery shirts and torn jeans. Some of them played the guitar, others drank cans of beer, or whisky straight from the bottle. My mother purred. When she wanted to be alone with them, she sent us to our room.

Pablito and I are lying on the bed. We've pulled the blanket over us to keep warm. Huddled against each other, we stare silently at the ceiling. Outside the door we hear raised voices.

'Come on, Philippe, play something for us!'

That's Lili, the downstairs neighbour and a friend of my mother's.

We hear a high-pitched, dissonant chord on the guitar, then a falsetto, whining voice singing a Nat King Cole song.

'How about something less sentimental? How about some flamenco? Pablo adores flamenco!'

That voice, of course, is my mother's, with her 'Pablo adores the guitar', 'Pablo loves this', 'Pablo loves that', or 'That's no way to talk to Pablo's daughter-in-law!', 'I've seen it all. I'm a Picasso!'

And they keep swigging the whisky and guzzling the beer. There's Lili's coarse laughter and my mother's, and the laughter of the men that, tucked away in our room, Pablito and I call the 'yobs', and whom we don't like.

At seven in the morning we have to get up to go to school. Our mother is still asleep.

The kitchen is a mess. The table is littered with glasses, bottles and overflowing ashtrays. Without a word, we clear the table, wipe the oilcloth clean with a sponge, throw away the cigarette-ends and empty bottles, and put the glasses in the sink.

If we want our mother to be nice, our father to smile and our grandfather to love us, we must make them forget that we're a burden. After all, it's our fault that our father demeans himself for his weekly allowance, that grandfather often refuses to see us, and that our mother brings home yobs. If we weren't around, everyone could live in peace. Everyone could be happy.

Knowing what a burden we were, Pablito and I thought we might be capable of bringing the good guy (my father) and the bad guy (my grandfather) together, and getting them to make up.

We called it 'building happiness'. It consisted of cleaning the house, tidying our room, washing the dishes, and serving my mother breakfast in bed.

I still remember how terrified I was as I stood on a chair and lit a match to heat up the water on the old gas stove. I was afraid of scalding myself as I poured the water into my mother's special cup. And yet we loved bringing the tea to her.

She would barely open her eyes and say, 'Not now, children. I'm sick. I have to sleep.'

We didn't realize then that her problem was drink-related, and called a 'hangover'. Worried, we asked what was wrong.

'It comes from the tuberculosis I had as a child . . .'

Or: 'My pancreas is acting up again.'

We tiptoed out of the room so she could go back to sleep and get over her pain.

We had to go to school.

Now that I've crossed the Rubicon thanks to analysis, I have a new way of looking at things that I didn't have when I was bringing up Gaël and Flore, my two oldest children. I had a desperate and passionate love for them, a love that was animal-like. I try to give my adopted children, May, Dimitri and Florian, a love that will help them, first of all, to shape their own identity. I am there every morning, before they go to school, to make sure they've brushed their teeth, put on good shoes and dressed warmly. I make them eat breakfast, quiz them on their school work, and check their school bags or their sports kit. This may seem excessive, but these are gestures of love that I didn't receive and I'm attached to them.

3

Primary school, at break-time. The plane trees are decked in autumn colours. The boys and girls are frolicking about, twittering and chirping like birds in an aviary. The teachers pace up and down the playground gently trying to maintain a semblance of order and discipline. We have started a game of marbles. Not the kind 'for weaklings' but the real thing: a marble is held inside the fist and the thumb is whipped out like a spring to propel it against the marble of one or more opponents. We use large marbles made of plaster or glass. Each kid for himself, no cheating allowed, 'cross my heart and hope to die', may the best one win . . .

I'm one of the best in the class at this game. Squatting, so concentrated as to almost give myself cramp, I defend my honour − the honour of a champion, of '*La Picasso*'. My classmates cheer me on with their southern accents, redolent of thyme and garlic.

'Go on, *La Pi-ca-sso*! Roll the orange one!'

'*La Picasso*.' No connection with my grandfather, who is in all the newspapers, no connection with my mother, who revels in outrageous behaviour. I'm anonymous and so is Pablito. In his grey dungarees, he cheers me on and picks up the marbles I win. We're as happy as urchins.

Finally content to be family-less.

As we are counting our winnings in a corner of the playground, two older kids come and stand in front of us.

'Is it true,' the first kid asks, 'that you come to school with a chauffeur and bodyguard? Is it true that you're rich?'

Chauffeur, bodyguard and rich? This morning we left the house on an empty stomach.

The second kid is short, fat and pimply; he pulls a sheet of paper covered in scrawls out of his school bag.

'Look,' he says, waving the paper under my nose, 'I can make Picassos too.'

My hackles up, I challenge him. 'Say that again!'

He sniggers and taunts me, 'I'm as good as Picasso. It's just scribbles.'

I see red. Seething with anger that this dimwit has the nerve to attack my grandfather, I punch him in the face. His mouth starts to bleed.

An energetic hand grabs me by the arm — it's the teacher. She shakes me and shouts in my ear, 'Go and stand in the corner!'

His chin quivering, Pablito cuts in, 'But Miss, he started it.'

'I don't want to get into it,' says the teacher, fuming. 'Both you and your sister will write out the sentence "I must not fight with my school mates" twenty times.'

What could I have said or done then to convince people that I wasn't trying to defend Picasso, nor the pride of the Picassos, but my whole family? That it was love that drove me to use my fists. A love that my family didn't give me but that I yearned for – just a friendly pat on the head, a caress, a kiss on the cheek, some sign of affection. If my grandfather's name had been Smith instead of Picasso, I would have risen to the defence of my grandfather Smith. If he'd been a house painter and repainted our school, I would have fought for the same reason . . .

But it's best to shut up and not to think about it, because it's not nice to try to imagine other things than what life gives us.

> *I must not fight with my schoolmates*
> *You must not fight with your schoolmates*
> *He must not fight with his schoolmates . . .*

Seated in front of what remains of the meal that our mother has left for us, we set to work on our punishment. We haven't touched the saucepan of congealed ratatouille and barely eaten the slice of ham, which we have carefully replaced in its greaseproof paper.

Our mother has left us a note on the table saying she had to go to Cannes. Why? That's none of our business.

During my analysis, tears used to stream down my face as I relived those solitary meals. Other children would come home from school to find a welcoming house and an attentive mother. I can't remember my exact words, but I know I talked about wanting to have had a mother who made time for her children, who pampered them, listened to their problems, and nourished them, even with a badly cooked meal. Like those mashed potatoes that she used to burn . . . and that were delicious.

Not long ago I read about a scientist who had conducted a sad experiment. He had separated two baby mice from their mother and put them in a labyrinth leading to two separate enclosures. One enclosure was heated and lined with fur, the other was cold but included a pipette from which milk dripped. Two weeks later, the mice were found dead in the heated enclosure. The other enclosure was clean and deserted. The milk had curdled.

Pablito and I had no such choice. The warm enclosure lined with fur, which our mother offered us, was too dependent on the Picasso enclosure that provided milk – milk paid for at too high a price.

I remember the days when we would come home from school and open the front door in trepidation. In what state would we find our mother? Sick in bed, or wound up like a mechanical toy whose frenzied chatter increasingly embarrassed us with each passing day.

'I'm sure Picasso would like my décolletage', 'I'm the kind of woman Picasso is crazy about', 'If Picasso doesn't want to see me it's because of your father' . . . And indirectly, 'because of you.'

It was because of us that my father had to beg for money. Because of us that my mother was a fantasist, because of us that they had divorced. Because of us that my grandfather excluded us from his life.

There isn't a single hint of our existence in his work, not one drawing or painting. When we went to La Californie, we would search for ourselves desperately on the walls, secretly flipping through the catalogues and art books, trying to find our features in a faun, a bacchanal, or the kaleidoscope of a still life. We came across studies and paintings of Maya, Picasso's daughter with Marie-Thérèse Walter; sketches and portraits of Claude and Paloma, his children with Françoise Gilot; of fishermen, his tailor, people we didn't know, dogs, cats, birds, lobsters, guitars, coffee pots, fruit bowls, jugs, leeks . . . but not a single sketch of us, his direct heirs.

We might have offered an interesting theme, if he had ever bothered to think about our despair. Just think: 'Pablito and Marina chased from La Californie', 'Pablito with tear-filled eyes', 'Marina and Pablito clinging to each other'.

Despite the fact that we visited him at La Californie, came to see him in the château de Vauvenargues, and went to so many bullfights with him, he chased us from his palette. To him, we were transparent.

I think we were an obstacle to Picasso's well-being. The offspring of a disappointing father and an outrageous mother, the fact that we existed disturbed him. We disrupted his genius, his painter's nirvana.

Though they were aware of our suffering, neither my father nor my mother had the courage to say to us, 'There are no drawings of you because your grandfather wants to punish us – not you – for the bickering and arguments we had when we separated. They reminded him all too vividly of his own failed relationships with his various women.'

Today, I would say that this 'punishment' allows me to distance myself from my grandfather and loudly proclaim that the only, magnificent creation he gave us – and it is dearest to me – was the birth of my father.

Even if he was absent.

The streets of Golfe-Juan are decorated with garlands, the shop windows are glittering, the pavements jammed with people. The shops overflow with gifts, and piped carols come from the loudspeakers nestled in the branches of the plane trees . . . Christmas is two days away.

When we bring my mother her cup of tea, she opens

her eyes and, before going back to sleep, mumbles, 'Your father called. He's going to try and stop by to give you Picasso's present.'

Picasso's present. Our only one, given jointly by my grandfather, my father and my mother. The necessary, sacrosanct gift, chosen in the fashionable shops of Cannes by Picasso's secretaries, who don't know us, to suit the all-powerful image of the great master. For me, a silk scarf from Hermes or a valuable doll from a well-known antique shop. For Pablito, a silver chain-bracelet or a tie-pin. Gifts that have no heart or soul. A bureaucratic chore for my grandfather's flunkeys who, by fiddling the price in each shop, give themselves a Christmas bonus behind their boss's back.

My father drops by for a quick visit. For once my mother daren't harass him or shower him with reproaches. He put the presents on the table and waits religiously for Pablito and me to remove the extravagant ribbons and wrappings.

My box contains a silver pen and a lead pencil, Pablito's a leather wallet with his initials.

'Once again, your grandfather has spoilt you,' my father exclaims.

'These are valuable objects,' says my mother. 'I'll give them to you when you're older.'

Back in our room, Pablito and I try to amuse ourselves. Pablito is playing Cowboys and Indians with his toy soldiers and I'm playing with Lélanta, the doll my grandmother Olga gave me a long time ago. Lélanta is my friend in adversity. In the summer I take her to the beach or to the Iles de Lérins. She swims with me in the rocky inlets where I like to bathe, dries off in the sun, and becomes my confidante. At home, when dark thoughts haunt me, I pack her clothes in a little suitcase, hold her in my arms and whisper into her ear, 'Come on, let's go and live our own life.'

We only ever get to the end of the Rue Chabrier; this little taste of freedom is immediately spoilt by guilt at the thought of deserting my mother, and especially Pablito.

I also like to perform operations on Lélanta. I cut her belly open with a kitchen knife and empty out her stuffing. My brother helps me, directing me and offering his diagnosis: 'Surely a case of nerves,' he says solemnly. 'We must extract the problems that are torturing her.'

The problems that were torturing us.

When we were small children, Christmas always included my grandmother Olga. Even though I was little, I knew that, on that day, as on Sundays, she would come by coach from Cannes, eat lunch with us and leave before nightfall. She always brought a small Christmas tree wrapped in newspaper to keep its needles from shedding. She would unwrap the tree in front of us, hang some small ornaments and garlands on it – which she magically took out of her bag – and set it up in a corner of our room. Then she would give each of us a present – a box of soldiers and some toy cars for Pablito and, for me, a stuffed animal or a doll – a real one I could hug and play with without having to wash my hands.

I will always think of my grandmother Olga as the ideal grandmother. She was a kind of magician who had a gift for smoothing out difficulties, taming my mother's demons, enhancing my father's image, and bringing us peace and harmony. We liked the fragrance of her eau de toilette, her melodious accent, her elegant gestures, her kind eyes and her respect for others.

Later, when we went to see her in the clinic where she spent the last days of her life, I never heard her say a negative word about my grandfather. She only said that he was her husband, that he was a very great artist, and that some day we would be as great as he. When Pablito used to explain to her that he was tired of hearing people call him 'Picasso's *petit-fils*' ('grandson' but also 'small son'), as a joke on grandfather's small size, she replied, 'Right now you're the small son of the great painter but soon you'll be the great son of the small painter.'

She was attentive to my mother's grievances, agreed tacitly with everything she said, and offset her emotionalism with level-headed advice.

'Take courage, Mienne. Things will work out.'

She knew how to respond to all the quandaries of life.

I was very fortunate to have had her as a grandmother. She was a wonderful woman and it was wrong of certain people to tarnish her image just to flatter Picasso's ego. It would be too great an honour to name these people, who did so much harm to the only woman who really loved Picasso. Thank God I don't belong to that clan of 'experts' who tear my grandmother to shreds in order to glorify Picasso's work, that I am not part of their servile cult. When I hear them talk about Picasso's genius, I'm tempted to reply, 'Yes, a genius for cruelty.'

Olga Kokhlova was born on 17 June 1891 in Nezhin, in the Ukraine. She was the daughter of a colonel in the imperial army. Passionate about dance in a milieu where it was disapproved of, she waited until she came of age, then broke off with her family to join Diaghilev's Ballets Russes and travel with the company all over the world.

The Great War, the Russian Revolution, her marriage to Picasso meant that she would never return to her native land.

Everyone who has written about Picasso claims that my grandmother wasn't a good dancer. But if this were true, why would Sergey Diaghilev, who was uncompromising in his choice of male and female dancers, have kept my grandmother in his company? It can't have been to sleep with her, because he was only attracted to men.

I know that my grandfather loved her. Fascinated by her beauty, captivated by her grace, he had wooed her in vain in Rome, Naples and Barcelona where the Ballets Russes were performing with stage sets he had designed. Rejecting his advances, she imposed a slower courtship on him than he had been accustomed to with his previous girlfriends. When he had introduced her to his mother in Barcelona, she had warned Olga, 'No woman can ever be happy with my son Pablo.' It was a futile warning: Diaghilev and his company left for South America and Olga decided not go with them. Picasso had won her heart. He gave her a proper wedding at the Russian Orthodox church on Rue Daru in Paris.

Marriage to Olga allowed Picasso – a man who liked to settle scores – to forget the social milieu of his childhood in Malaga, which he was so ashamed of.

Olga has been called snobbish and frivolous but, in marrying her, Picasso was also banking on what she had to offer. She would enable him to get closer to a world that he didn't know – the high-society world of aristocratic taste and *savoir-vivre*. He bought his clothes in London, learned to drink champagne, haunted fashionable salons and aped the bourgeoisie, whom he had hitherto always maligned.

So who was frivolous and snobbish, Olga or Picasso?

At the end of her life, Olga Kokhlova had a stroke and her legs were paralysed. Nevertheless she refused to be taken around in a wheelchair. For a dancer, being in a wheelchair is the ultimate punishment, a terrible insult. When we went to see her in the Beausoleil Clinic where I was born and she would die, she would sit on her bed to receive us, her legs covered by her mink coat, a memento from the happy days when Picasso loved her. Pablito would insist on wearing a velvet blazer and trousers for our visits that made him look like a little prince. She inspired a taste for elegance in him without her saying anything. She would ask us to sit beside her on the bed and, taking both our hands in hers, she would tell us stories in Russian, which we couldn't understand but found beautiful.

They were our special secret.

People have talked about Olga and her jealousy, Olga and her hysterics, Olga and her ravings – no one has minced words. True, Picasso threw her to the lions: he talked of finding her exasperating, stupid, annoying and frivolous.

He lacked chivalry, to say the least, in depicting himself as her victim, blackening the woman he had loved, and fomenting his son's ill will towards his mother. And then, to make matters worse, he broadcast the fact that Marie-Thérèse Walter, tired of being kept behind the scenes, had turned up on Olga's doorstep to inform her that the baby in her arms was 'the work of Picasso' . . .

My grandmother has been called an hysteric, but consider how dishonoured, humiliated and demeaned she was. It is not easy to recover from so much cruelty, baseness and disillusionment.

Broken by her many years of grief, my grandmother took leave of this world on 11 February 1955 with the dignity that was characteristic of her. My father wanted to be alone at her funeral. Most probably to be forgiven for the harm he had done her. And to tell her he loved her . . . In spite of the man who had ruined both their lives.

4

Geneva, 1982. Frédérique, my friend in need when I felt like I was dying, and now the ally in my new life, stops her car in front of the analyst's door. I am seeing him for the first time and I'm terrified.

Frédérique puts her hand on my arm. 'It will be fine,' she says.

I get out of the car like an automaton, quickly enter the unfamiliar building, take the lift and step out in front of an open door. How did I end up in this waiting room, with its impersonal furniture? I don't know . . . and I'm cold.

A stern–looking man is standing in front of me. I didn't see him walk in. He must be my analyst. I must introduce myself. Instead of saying, 'I am Marina Picasso,' the words that come out of my mouth are, 'I'm Picasso's grand-daughter.' I don't have an identity of my own. I am and will always be 'Picasso's granddaughter.'

He leads me to his office, asks me to sit down and observes me. Then he questions me. I answer in a very thin voice. After an hour of conversation punctuated by interminable silences, he offers to start working with me on the basis of five sessions a week. The only condition is that I come to my appointments by myself.

The dizzying trip to his office was a Calvary. The sprawling streets, the red traffic-lights ambushing me at the crossroads, the roar of the cars overtaking mine, my panic at having to park and continue on foot; and then the pavement shifting with every step, the abysses of street corners, the alarming buildings threatening to collapse on me. I feared the void and was terrified that I might be trapped in this neighbourhood where I was always getting lost. It was a heroic journey for me, through all kinds of obstacles: pedestrian crossings that had to be negotiated according to a precise ritual, lines on the pavement that were not be stepped on ... for fear of falling into a vacuum and losing my soul.

Finally, I would reach the entrance with its ancient stonework, the lift that jolted slightly at every floor, the metallic doors that opened with a gentle hiss, the dimly lit landing and the door with the doorbell, and over the doorbell, the discreet business card: 'P. A. Duvanel.'

I was afraid and bathed in sweat.

I am on the couch. Monsieur Duvanel — at first I used to call him Doctor — is sitting behind me. I'm glad I don't have to look into his eyes. I'm so ashamed of myself.

I stare at the bookshelves where I see symmetrical rows of books, a few statuettes, a photograph of Françoise Dolto, the child psychoanalyst. I'm unable to utter a word. Duvanel respects my silence, a silence full of stifled cries and unshed, suffocating tears. Then far away, behind me, I hear his voice. 'That will be all for today, Madame.'

The conversation has lasted twenty minutes — a silent conversation. I start to sob.

Three months of silence and of tears – a torrent of water shifting tons and tons of mud. My mother, my father, Picasso, Pablito's suffering, and my grandmother's, were all part of that viscous, sticky, repulsive mud: my father and his servility, my missing grandfather, the lost look in Pablito's eyes in the hospital, my grandmother with her legs hidden under her mink coat.

They were all dead. The only survivor: my neurotic, deranged mother.

And I too am deranged as I lie on this austere couch, where I die with each word I utter.

Words. Some make love and others make war. Amnesia, slips of the tongue, screen memories, metaphors, truth, falsehood, identification, free association: '*mer* and *mère*' (sea and mother), '*ciel* and *fiel*' (heaven and gall), '*amour, mort*' (love, death) . . . Words are live creatures.

Meanwhile I have to wait for the tangled knot of pain in my stomach to be extirpated . . . 'Kindly elaborate.' The pain has to be confronted directly. 'It was at La Californie . . .'

Soon I switch to the present tense: 'I am at La Californie . . . with my father . . . He's walking up and down . . . pouring himself a glass of . . .'

Suddenly I'm in a black hole. I can't remember what I have just said.

'That will be all for today, Madame.'

Some of the sessions take me back to the bullfights we used to go to with my grandfather. I sat next to him, terrified by the noise, the colours and the savagery of the *aficionados* shouting for the *faena*, the moment when the bull is put to death.

I sided with the bull.

On the analyst's couch, before I can recover the right to live, I must work through my own execution . . .

So many lances pierced my skin in that arena. How I butted against the cul-de-sac of my life, smashing the *callejón* boards. And all those *banderillas* that harpooned me in mid-charge, all those death-blows that drew streams of blood from my burning lungs. Now I know, I was a *toro bravo*. This is what Picasso shouted when the bull put up an heroic fight, before the horses dragged the corpse out of the arena to make way for another.

I was a *toro bravo*.

5

When our grandmother passed away, neither Pablito nor I cried. Our grief was beyond tears. We would never again see her smile, or hear her reassuring words. Never again experience her kindness, or those delightful moments by her bedside, drinking tea. 'Pablito, a drop of milk? Marina, a slice of lemon?'

I can still taste that tea; it tastes of a lost paradise.

There was also anger, anger at Picasso for never coming to ask her forgiveness when she was bedridden and in pain, even though he lived very close to the nursing home where she spent the last days of her life.

Hadn't his paintbrushes reminded him of how magnificent and regal she had been when she posed for him? Egoism, heartlessness, cowardliness, barbarity; he repudiated her after having glorified her so often in his paintings: 'Olga à la mantille', 'Olga au col de fourrure', 'Olga lisant', 'Olga pensive', not to mention many other Olgas, including the 'Olga dans un fauteuil' that lights up the hall of my house – a noble, enigmatic Vesta watching over me and my children.

When that magnificent woman died, everything

collapsed for Pablito and me. We were left alone with a father who came by to see us like a shooting star, and a mother who was wasting her life.

Since the 'Picasso allowance' that our mother received from our father was shrinking, she came up with the idea of suing Picasso. It was all very well for my father to turn down his mother's legacy so the Picasso oeuvre could remain intact, my mother saw no reason why she had to bear the brunt of this generosity. Convinced that she was within her rights, she proclaimed loudly to anyone who would listen that she had finally succeeded in muzzling the Minotaur, the lord and master of La Californie.

Her lawsuit and gossiping merely resulted in my grandfather turning against her even more. He hired a team of lawyers to fight her. His objective was to take us away from our mother and put us in a boarding school until we came of age.

When my mother spoke about this lawsuit – and she did so constantly – it took on fantastic proportions. She made herself into a crusading heroine, a *mater dolorosa* who was fighting to save her children.

'Picasso isn't equipped to have you live with him,' she said. 'He'll put you in private schools for the wealthy.'

Private schools for the wealthy – these words echoed in our minds like a damnation.

Then she added, ruthlessly, 'He'll separate you. You, Pablito, you'll end up in Spain and you, Marina, in the Soviet Union, with his communists . . . You won't see each other any more.'

Were Spain and the Soviet Union neighbouring countries? Would we be torn away from each other? We were practically twins; geography was like an ogre that devoured our hearts. We were terrified of it.

I don't know the details of what happened, but my mother won the battle, in spite of the odds stacked against her. She wanted her children and she got custody of them. The only other thing she won from Picasso was the appointment of a social worker responsible for checking up on our living conditions.

Glued to our mother's side, we watch the social worker's every move. She opens the fridge to see what it contains, checks our exercise books, inspects our wardrobe, and quizzes us on life with our mother. We are lawbreakers subjected to a court ruling.

'What did you eat for lunch? What time did you go to bed?'

We lower our eyes, afraid of answering.

The social worker's name is Madame Boeuf. She's a pretty redhead. Occasionally she smiles at us and, on one occasion, she gives me a sweet.

'Why do you come and ruin all our Thursdays?' I ask her, tearfully.

She crouches down in front of me, looks into my eyes and says, 'I cross my heart, Marina dear, I won't ruin your Thursdays any more.'

We become friends and I find I can explain a lot of things to her.

'Madame Boeuf, I like the character of Silly Goose in the story.'

She looks at me wide-eyed but lets me speak.

'You know, Silly Goose is a simple person, but she's not stupid. She knows a lot, but she's usually unlucky. When she tries to go mountain climbing she always falls down.

She doesn't do it to make people laugh, she just can't climb the mountain. If people would listen to Silly Goose, they would realize that she's got lots of potential. She would be intelligent if she wasn't asked to climb those horrible mountains . . .'

Then I fall silent. Grown-ups don't really understand about life.

In those days Thursday was a day off from school. It was the only day when we felt free. We would get up very early, jump into our clothes and run out to join our friends in the street. Sometimes, Madame Alzeari or Lili would stop us as we ran by and give us a slice of cake or a sweet. They knew our mother had no desire to bake cakes and even less desire to squander money on sweets. We would thank them, with our mouths full. Then we would cycle down to the beach, followed by a gang of kids from the Rue Chabrier.

My bicycle was the equivalent, for me, of my father's Norton Manx motorbike. I would jump on and, standing on the pedals, zip straight down to the landing pier in the harbour, braking at the very last minute with a screech of tyres, two inches away from the end. Since we only had one bike between us, Pablito would sometimes borrow it from me when he wanted to pedal cautiously along the waterfront. I was more daredevil than he.

I also liked to jump into the sea. I swam doggy paddle, but extremely well. I loved swimming out to the open sea, beyond the area demarcated for swimming by buoys. It made me feel free from my mother and father's world and – small revenge – from the realm of Picasso, who was afraid when he couldn't touch the bottom.

I remember too the small boat that we appropriated and

made seaworthy. It was an old, sea- and sand-worn dinghy, a wreck abandoned to its fate by fishermen. With a few boards, four nails, some tar and a coat of paint – unearthed God knows where – my friends and I patched it up so it could float. We would take turns going on board, two or three at a time, rarely more, row like galley-slaves, bale out like maniacs and swim back after having sunk a few yards from the shore. The odyssey itself was unimportant, what counted was the dream – the dream of going very far away, beyond the horizon, with my travelling companions Pablito and Alain, a friend who was as mixed up as we were.

My father left a message saying he would try to stop by. He'd been trying to stop by for three months. Madame Boeuf said this was nothing to worry about, we had to wait for things to get better. It was all very well to wait for things to get better, but my mother couldn't, as she put it, make ends meet. She was greeted coldly by the butcher and the grocer when she asked them if she could put off paying them. We had to listen, of course, to her everlasting complaints.

'I bleed myself to bring you up while your father is out having a good time. He couldn't care less that I'm worried. And Picasso wouldn't care less if I fell ill . . .'

We were brought up on the words 'ill' and 'worried'. That's what life seemed to be all about.

The lean times stretched for days, weeks, months. We had to be careful about everything.

'Pablito, take care of your clothes. Marina, don't ruin your shoes. For dessert, you can share a banana.'

Irregular meals, unbuttered toast dipped in warm milk, scrambled eggs with tomato, pasta with meagre sauces, poor-man's rice. When you're a child, skipping a meal is not important so long as you know you're loved. It's much worse to be suffocated by a mother's endless pontifications. Between mouthfuls, ours would dispense her knowledge like a tyrant. She would interrupt us, speak for us, and inflict her theories on everything.

'Melon and strawberries are the best fruits . . . I love pink. Picasso used to tell me that it suited my complexion . . . I only like short skirts . . . I only like big breasts. Picasso likes short skirts too . . . and big breasts . . . That Algerian war is dragging on. Not surprising with the National Liberation Front that Picasso supports . . .'

A string of inanities spoilt the moments we spent together.

What happiness to get down from the table, with June heralding the holidays, the beach, the bike, the dinghy, our friends . . . and our mother delighted to be able to lie on the beach again in her bikini with her bunch of yobs.

We were happy in spite of her – in spite of everything.

The telephone rings in the night. Jolted awake, Pablito and I hold our breath. We know it's our father. He must be calling from a bar, like he usually does. Three, four rings, then silence. My mother picks up the phone in her room.

'Do you think he wants to see us?' Pablito whispers.

I don't say anything. I'd like it to be true.

We're up early in the morning and busy tidying the kitchen: there are dishes to be washed, the floor to be mopped, and laundry to be put out to dry on the balcony. Then we have to prepare our mother's breakfast – lay out the cup, the teapot and the sugar on a tray. No, no sugar, sugar is fattening. We look at the clock. It's nine. We have two hours to kill before waking her.

So we wait, not daring to move.

It *was* our father who called.

'He's remembered that he has children,' grumbles my mother. 'He said he would come by and pick you up.'

'When?'

'At one o'clock. Downstairs.'

Downstairs, because he is no longer allowed to come up. We can't show him our room ever again – the fortified castle Pablito has built in a shoebox, our exercise books, the drawings we've put up on the walls. He's an undesirable. We will never share our child's world with him again.

La Californie, the wait in front of the gate, the old concierge's footsteps, the key in the lock and the cutting words: 'You have an appointment?'

We cross the gravelled courtyard to the front steps; there we're met by the watchdog, Jacqueline Roque.

'Monseigneur is taking his shower. Go and play in the garden while you wait.'

Her tone of voice is gruff and arrogant. She's the mistress of the place. We must obey.

Pablito and I walk hand in hand, followed by the dachshund Lump. We don't dare run or talk to each other. Monseigneur is taking his shower. We must not disturb that solemn moment.

Our father is right behind us, a cigarette in his mouth. Shoulders hunched, he walks among the statues. Casually, he picks a sprig of lavender and puts it to his nose. Does its scent remind him of his childhood? Of a time when Picasso still respected him?

I abandon Pablito to join my father and slip my hand into his. I love him. He's my father.

In the studio my grandfather welcomes us in his cotton underpants, his overflowing attributes visible – an affront to me, as a little eight-year-old girl, and later as a seventeen-year-old, whom he will receive in the same way at the end of his life.

Was it an affront or a provocation? No, it was simply that he wasn't embarrassed to show himself this way in front of me, the cook or the young cleaning woman. His sexual organ was like his paintbrushes, the fish-bones piled up on his plate, Esméralda's droppings, or the piles of rusting tin cans heaped up on the ground. Cock, paintbrushes, fish-bones, droppings, rusted cans were part of his work. Everyone had to accept this – even if it was shocking.

The date, the fig, the walnut, consecrated by his fingers, a huge roar of laughter, and then a lesson in life, absurd and irrational.

'Children, you should know that one can do without everything and live very well – without shoes, clothes, even food. Look at me, I don't need anything.'

Pablito and I blush to the roots of our hair. Has our mother sent him a letter of complaint? Will he refuse to give my father his allowance? Once again, we feel guilty for existing.

Yet it's true he doesn't need anything, with his torn sailor's jersey, his ill-adjusted underpants, his worn espadrilles. What do we have to complain about? Our grandfather is like us. A pauper. The only difference is, he has a pile of money, whereas we'll be eating pasta again tonight.

'The important thing,' he adds, radiant, 'is to do what you feel like doing.'

The statement hits my father like a slap in the face. He lowers his eyes and stammers, 'Pablo, I've brought the paintings you wanted back from Paris. They're in the car.'

47

Side-stepping, evasiveness and fear: once again he is afraid of displeasing the powerful Minotaur, the *deus ex-machina* of his pitiful destiny.

Grandfather does not react. He merely smiles.

'Paulo,' he says finally, 'Next Sunday Dominguin will be fighting a bull in Arles. You'll come with me.'

And then, turning towards us, he adds, 'Bring Pablito and Marina if you want. After all, they have Spanish blood.'

The visit is over. Gratefully Pablito and I thank our grandfather for a wonderful day. He leans down towards us, accepts our kisses and exclaims with a laugh, '*Hasta la vista, muchachos! A domingo próximo!*'

We walk towards the metal gate, where my father is unloading the paintings from the boot of the Oldsmobile. He carries them into the house and asks us to wait quietly.

He returns with a spring in his step and a happy expression. Evidently, my grandfather has been charitable – not with his heart but with his money.

That evening in Golfe-Juan we eat pizza from Da Luigi's, the trattoria in the harbour.

A slice of luxury.

6

The best visits to La Californie were when my father was relaxed and my grandfather happy. Holding each other in a warm *abrazo*, they talked about Spain, about cousins who still lived there, and made travel plans.

Pablito and I would hold our breath, afraid of dispelling the happiness.

When we were little we were part of what grandfather called 'the gang': Paloma and Claude (Françoise Gilot's children), Catherine Hutin (Jacqueline Roque's daughter) and us, Paulo's children. We were all about the same age, give or take two or three years; an uncle, two aunts, a niece and a nephew all still in short trousers and all making mischief in the anarchic disorder of La Californie. We played hopscotch on the mosaic in the hall, tag around the trees and statues in the garden, hide-and-seek amongst the junk in the studio, and run boisterous races up the stairs. Our rowdiness was egged on by Picasso – father to some, grandfather to others. A playmate to all of us.

Those moments seemed magical to me. We were finally recognized and accepted. When we drew lots for a game of blindman's-buff and it was my turn to be blindfolded,

I was so unwilling to lose sight even momentarily of the miracle that I used to yell, 'Leave me alone, I don't want to not see.'

Not to want to not see – two negatives equal an affirmation. I wanted to collect every crumb of an exceptional happiness.

This was the blessed time when Paloma and Claude were still allowed at La Californie, before their mother decided to unlock the cage in which Picasso had kept her for too long. When Pablito and I had not yet witnessed the violent clashes between our mother and father. The blessed time when we were able to be just children.

Sometimes we would all spend the night together in a room converted into a dormitory. But it was never more than one night. Our presence disrupted Picasso's work and disturbed Jacqueline Roque. She wanted to be alone with her Monseigneur, in the golden prison she was building around him.

But there were still visits where Pablito and I tried not to give any sign of our existence. These were the visits where my father was reproached by his father in front of us: 'You don't know how to bring them up,' 'They need a responsible father' . . .

I found these arbitrary sermons degrading and my father's behaviour towards his executioner pitiful. As a form of escapism, I concentrated my thoughts on the sea, the sun, the beach, my friends and the old dinghy. I made up an imaginary fisherman father who would take me out on the open sea every day and sell his daily catch at the market. I made up an imaginary mother who would be ready to clean houses rather than be dependent on Picasso – and a Picasso who would be a real grandfather . . .

I made up parents who were not part of the world that had been chosen for me.

I remember Sundays when Catherine Hutin would tell us about the school where her mother had enrolled her as a boarder so that 'Monseigneur' would not be disturbed. Since she knew nothing else of life, she turned her little room into a pretend classroom. An inflexible teacher with a wheedling smile, she would hit our fingers with a ruler.

Perhaps inflicting this punishment on us was her way of relieving her resentment against Picasso, who didn't want her to live at La Californie.

I also remember the day when, to my amazement, I saw my grandfather look sad for the first time. I had wanted to check how many minutes were left before Jacqueline Roque – by then Madame Picasso – would inform us that the visit was over, and, without thinking, I had consulted the watch my mother had given me in a recent burst of generosity. My grandfather suddenly looked pained. 'Are you bored?' he asked.

For the first time, he seemed genuinely hurt, like a real grandfather.

I didn't want to break the spell, so I didn't answer. I was afraid that the Picasso who was inconvenienced by us would resurface and drive away the flash of affection that I still have engraved in my memory.

To get away from La Californie, which had been desecrated by developers who had built a block of flats on the edge of its grounds, obstructing the view of the sea and the Iles de Lérins, my grandfather bought a Provençal farmhouse in Mougins: Notre-Dame-de-Vie.

Notre-Dame-de-Vie was a veritable bunker protected by electrified railings and barbed wire. Visitors were filtered at the entrance by an intercom system, and Afghan hounds, trained to attack, roamed the grounds day and night. At Notre-Dame-de-Vie, our visits were quickly turned into official interviews, carefully timed by the implacable Jacqueline, guardian of the sanctuary.

Was Picasso aware of the wall she had erected? I'm afraid he was. He alone had the authority to confer this power on her while remaining in the background.

Both bitter and hurt about Françoise Gilot's book, *Life with Picasso*, he no longer saw Claude and Paloma, nor, for petty reasons, Maya, his daughter with Marie-Thérèse Walter. Only my father was still admitted and my father insisted that Pablito and I go with him to demonstrate that he took care of us. He never allowed us to see our grandfather without his being present. The iron curtain drawn between grandfather and us was heavy – and hermetically sealed against our questions, our desires, our suffering.

What had become of the light of La Californie? At Notre-Dame-de-Vie everything was gloomy: the funereal cypress trees, the lugubrious olive trees, the impregnable enclosure and the metallic voice emanating from the Cyclops eye of the intercom.

'Who is it?'

'It's Paulo. Paulo and the children.'

Silence, followed by: 'The Maître can't see you.'

A week later, another attempt answered by the same anonymous voice: 'The Maître is out . . .' or, 'The Maître is resting.'

'The Maître will see you.'

We are finally admitted into a kind of crypt with dry-stone walls: grandfather's studio. Jacqueline, priestess of the shrine, is there and so is Kaboul, one of the Afghan hounds.

'Be careful, he bites,' she says before slipping away like a shadow.

'Did I keep you waiting?'

This cheerless voice is my grandfather's. We didn't see him walk in. Did he drop from the sky?

'Hello, Pablo,' my father whispers. 'The children wanted to see you . . .'

Picasso greets us with his burning eyes.

Earlier, before Notre-Dame-de-Vie, there had been the château de Vauvenargues with its four towers and forty windows. I know because I counted them, with the mistral wind blowing through my hair, and my eyes squinting against the holiday sun. We went there when we accompanied grandfather and father to the grape-harvest bullfights in Arles. We sometimes went there without Picasso and, to scare us, our father would tell us that it was haunted by the ghost of its first owner, Luc de Clapiers, Marquis of Vauvenargues . . .

How could I have imagined that, on an April day in 1973, Picasso's ghost would join him there, at the foot of the Montagne Sainte-Victoire, a place infused by the memory of Cézanne?

Geneva and the couch, which is both rack and life raft. I'm crying. I only know how to cry and feel guilty.

'Why couldn't I see?'

Behind me, I hear the analyst's voice.

'Couldn't see? Be clear . . .'

I'm silent. How can I express the emotions that are battling within me? Regret, love and resentment.

I'm in pain.

Why didn't I understand that Picasso was indifferent to everything outside his work? His life didn't centre around Pablito or me, my father, my mother, my grandmother Olga, or the women whose deaths he brought about. There was only one thing that mattered to him: painting. In order to create, he had to destroy everything that got in the way of his creation.

'A painting,' he said to Christian Zervos, the founder of the art journal *Cahiers d'art*, 'is a series of additions. For me, a painting is a series of destructions.'

And here we were, longing for understanding – not knowing that he also had to destroy *us*.

'Monseigneur isn't here.'

Monseigneur *couldn't* be there – not for us. We were merely the fall-out from his art.

'That will be all for today, Madame.'

7

Arles. The cries of vendors running through the spectators hawking cushions – red, orange, purple, blue cushions that are snapped up by people who want to be more comfortably seated on the stone steps of the Roman amphitheatre. Other traders are selling ice-creams, doughnuts, peanuts and drinks. The crowd swarms and buzzes like bees, excited, fanatical; they have come to see blood flow.

In the arena, the *peones* are levelling the freshly watered ochre sand. It is the hour when the sun maps out the corners of shade and light in which the bull will choose to fight.

In the front row sit my grandfather, my father and Pablito. Three generations of Spaniards driven by the same passion – that of defying life and challenging death.

As for me, I don't exist.

Bullfights are a man's business.

At the top of the steps, the heralds blow their trumpets. This is the signal for the *alguacils*, two horsemen dressed in black in a style dating back to the reign of Philip II, to gallop across the ring and stop in front of the President's box. He gestures, giving them permission to open the bullfight. The crowd stands on the steps, cheering them.

The Picasso clan – Pablo, Paulo, Pablito – hasn't moved a muscle. One does not mix with the jubilant mob.

The procession begins to the sound of brass instruments. Three matadors emerge from passageway that leads to the horse enclosure and walk into the arena. With ceremonial capes draped over their left arms, they take small steps, chins raised and chests thrust out. The gold on their clothes sparkles in the sunlight.

The eyes of the Picasso men are burning with pleasure at being involved in the fight. They smile at each other.

'*Qué tal, Pablo*?' asks Paulo.

'*Muy bien, hijo*!' Luis–Miguel has promised me a good fight.'

Luis–Miguel Dominguin: the matador that all the *aficionados* have come specially to honour today. Dominguin, the man who has killed over two thousand bulls in his career. Luis–Miguel Dominguin whom the Picassos – Pablito included – joined this morning at the Hôtel Nord–Pinus while he put on his glittering attire (a favour reserved for family and close friends) before he secluded himself to implore the help of the Virgin and Saint Veronica.

'Before he dies gored by the bull,' adds Pablito with pride, looking into my eyes.

Dies with perforated guts and spurting blood.

Like my brother Pablito. Much later. In a completely different arena.

Behind the matadors – with Dominguin walking in the middle – are the twelve *banderilleros* and eight *picadors*, by order of seniority, on their caparisoned horses, miserable nags with crooked legs and lowered ears.

My eyes meet Picasso's. Impassible, he averts his gaze. My presence disturbs him.

'Why do you cry over the fate of those horses?' he asked me once. 'They're old and only good for the butcher's shop.'

This was when I understood that he wasn't interested in fate of those who served his pleasure. Their lives were secondary.

The parade is over. The *picadors* have left the arena. The attendants are levelling the sand stirred up by the horses' hooves. The *matadors* and their *cuadrillas*, or teams, have returned to their passageway, the *callejón*. While waiting to fight, they drape their heavy ceremonial capes over the fence protecting the first row of seats. Dominguin has sent his cape to Jacqueline Picasso; she is sitting in the second row next to Jean Cocteau, who has come specially from Saint-Jean-Cap-Ferrat. Dominguin then goes up to the *barrera* and selects a combat cape that is cherry red on the outside and yellow on the inside.

Picasso's eagle eye is recording every gesture. Tonight or tomorrow they will be reproduced on a canvas, a dish or, immediately after the fight, in that notebook he never parts with. My father avoids speaking to him. He knows that this transcendent moment must not be disturbed; it is like the moment Dominguin will experience just before the kill when he is cradled between the bull's horns.

Pablito also respects this mystery. His chin propped between his fists, he is staring at his grandfather.

At this moment, lost in their thoughts, they resemble each other so much . . . and also Dominguin who, behind his *burladero* – the wooden screen in the arena that provides the *matador* with a refuge – is bracing himself to face fear.

The door of the bull-pen releases its first bull and a tidal wave of violence sweeps through the ring. The bull churns the sand furiously with his hooves and collides head on with the boards of the *callejón*; he snorts, foams at the mouth and rears up. He's alone with his overwhelming rage, must save his own skin alone – just like Picasso when he burns with desire to attain the absolute through painting.

One of the *banderilleros* walks towards the bull, taunts him with his cape and forces him to charge. Behind his shelter, Dominguin studies the bull's leaps and his butting movements, evaluating its power, shortcomings and courage. His face twitches.

Now it's his turn to challenge – and honour – the animal. He walks into the arena with small, sliding steps. The bull stands firm. His muscles are tense and quivering. Dominguin provokes him head on. He stands utterly still as the bull swoops down on him and is engulfed in the folds of his cape. The right horn grazes Dominguin's chest. Beast and man are fused. Without flinching, the man performs his moves: *verónicas*, *manoletinas*, dangerous, faultless *parones*.

'*Olé!*'

'*Anda!*'

Everyone in the arena, the *plaza de toros*, is standing, their eyes glued to each pass.

Picasso is exultant and shouts himself hoarse: '*Para los pies! Anda, Luis Miguelito!*'

He leans towards Pablito and ruffles his hair. '*Niño*,' he says laughingly, '*parar, templar, mandar* are the three commandments of bullfighting. *Parar* is keeping your two feet still, *templar* is moving the material slowly, *mandar* is controlling the bull with the material . . .'

He turns towards Cocteau and calls out to him, pointing to my brother, 'You see, Jean, this one will be a *torero!*'

'*Parar, templar, mandar,*' Pablito stammers, starry-eyed. His grandfather has graced him with his attention. He must show himself worthy of it.

My father has moved closer to me. 'Is everything okay, Marina?'

I'm happy and I burst out laughing.

Everything's okay. I have a family.

A bugle call and the first act begins: *la suerte de varas* (the trial of the lances).

Booed by the crowd, the *picadors* make their entrance, paunchy and arrogant in their brocade tunics. Their horses, weighed down by their riders and their quilted covering, limp to their designated place for the fight — a path traced out with chalk on the sand. They are blindfolded.

'It's to calm them,' my father explains.

'When one is nothing, one doesn't look death straight in the face,' Picasso breaks in. The only death that counts in the arena is the bull's death.

Homage to the Minotaur who feeds off flesh.

In his shady corner, his *querencia*, the bull is digging up the sand with his hooves.

The *peones* rush towards the ring. Whirling their capes, they provoke, assail and goad the bull. The hysterical crowd spur them on and encourage the beast.

'*Anda toro! Anda!*'

The beast's nostrils are frothing with rage.

One *peon*, more daring than the others, ventures into the *querencia* where the beast has retreated.

Time stops.

The bull rises to his feet, sniffing the air and butting the sky. He charges, swift as lightning, evading the cape held out by the *peon*, then leaps round, back towards the cape, which brushes against his side.

In front of him the *picador* tries to keep his horse from rearing. A pause, a moment of reprieve, and then a new charge. The horse is lifted from the ground and forced against the *barrera*. He sinks down on to his front legs but still manages to remain upright. The bull tries to find a way to gore him through the protective padding on his flank. The *picador* sinks his lance into the bulge of muscle on the beast's neck. Red, terrifying blood gushes out. Once more a lance is thrown and once more the steel wounds the cornered animal. And once more . . . on and on. In bullfighting jargon this monstrosity is called the 'punishment.'

Punishment for what? For having allowed itself to be inhumanely trapped so that the men can demonstrate their barbarity, their will to power? So that they can feel important? To be depicted on a canvas one day: 'Still life with bull's skull', 'Guernica', 'Minotaur', 'Minotauromachy'?

Another bugle call is heard in the distance. The *picadors* have left the arena.

I feel crushed.

I have sustained too many lances.

I'm not interested in the rest of the fight. Nor am I interested in this audience of would-be gladiators: Picasso, who is being bombarded by photographers, my father, who is drinking his umpteenth can of beer, Cocteau, the magnificent buffoon, Jacqueline in her black shawl.

I feel the sting of the *banderilleros'* barbs. I wish the film could be run backwards: the blood on the bull's coat, the lances in his neck would disappear and he would recover all his glory. I wish the *barrera* and the stone steps would vanish into thin air, and that a strong gust of wind would blow away the *toreros* and their idolatrous audience. I wish the bull could be back in his field with his herd . . .

I wish this bullfight had never been.

On splayed legs, the bull awaits the final act: the *faena*, or kill.

Arrogantly, Dominguin turns his back on the animal and walks up to the steps. He takes off his head-dress, and brandishes it in Picasso's direction. He offers him death.

The crowd claps and roars, while Pablito squeezes up beside me.

I put my arm around his shoulders. I'm afraid too.

Inseparable, like those parakeets which can only live in couples, we are welded together, hand in hand, forehead against forehead. We refuse to take part in this ignominy.

We hear '*olé*'s and piercing whistles. We are paralysed by anxiety, as if brimstone were about to descend from the sky.

'Do you think he will suffer?' whispers Pablito.

Cheers, applause and the sound of bugles. Paulo and I raise our heads. In the arena, the bull's blood spills on to the ochre ground.

The bull is dead. Liberated.

A white handkerchief is waved from the presidential stand. At this signal, Dominguin goes up to the dead bull and slices off one of his ears. He throws it to my grandfather.

This blood-covered ear still haunts my nights. I have visions of it resting on the step where Pablito and I were sitting: the yellowish cartilage and tufts of hair sticky with blood.

A homage to my grandfather – the great *aficionado* of human distress.

— 8 —

After Arles we don't hear from our father for four months. Nor, of course, do we see our grandfather, for whom we are utterly insignificant.

Yet we are Picassos, Picassos like him. Picassos that people point out in the street.

'See that little boy and little girl? They are Picasso's grandchildren.'

'The multimillionaire painter?'

'Who else?'

The grandchildren of the multimillionaire painter are wandering the deserted streets of Golfe-Juan without a penny to their names.

It's the end of summer. The holiday-makers have left. The beach is deserted, the metal shutters of the restaurants drawn. The sun is behind cloud.

It's the beginning of the new school year.

Once again our mother has made a decision on our behalf. She has enrolled us at the Protestant school in Cannes.

'It's a highly respected school,' she says.

She has a reputation to maintain.

The alarm rings. It's half past six. Dazed and sleepy, I get up and shake Pablito.

'Hurry up, we're going to miss the bus.'

He gets up like a zombie, gropes for his shirt and trousers, puts them on half asleep and joins me in the bathroom. We wash as quietly as possible. Our mother is still asleep.

There's no time for breakfast. Just enough time to comb our hair, put on our shoes and slip thermoses into our satchels. These contain our midday meal, prepared the night before by Madame Danielle – the volunteer house-keeper who has been sent by the Social Services to help our mother with the household tasks. Today it is blanquette of veal.

'It's healthy and nourishing,' Madame Danielle said to my mother. 'I have made enough for two days.'

Between our textbooks and exercise books we've squeezed two paper plates, a metal tumbler, a knife and a fork. For dessert, an orange. Yesterday it was an apple.

We grab the key to the apartment from the table, quietly lock the door, and scramble down the stairs.

Day is just breaking.

I have bitter memories of those early mornings: the walk to the Route Nationale where the bus stopped, the refuse collectors in their truck emptying the dustbins, the level crossing with its siren announcing the arrival of a freight train. We trudged along, in all weathers, carrying our heavy satchels, the fear of being late in the pit of our stomachs.

I was also afraid of the crush of passengers in the packed bus to Cannes. At eight and ten years old we were too small to compete with their jostling, so we huddled up close to each other to minimize the amount of space we occupied. On bad days, the trip lasted forty-five minutes. When we arrived at Cannes station, we still had a twenty-minute walk to the Protestant school in Avenue de Grasse.

The school is called the 'school on the hill'. The teachers are nice; they like children. They never scold us. Charitable and humane, they sympathize with my mother's situation. They know that our father isn't around to take care of us and that our grandfather makes no effort to make the life of his grandchildren any easier. They don't sit in judgement, or label us. As far as they're concerned, we're no different from other children. We're Marina and Pablo. Pablo, not Pablito. Not Picassos. Following Protestant principles, they want us to be responsible for our actions and learn to be proud of ourselves. There are no chosen ones on this earth, there is just the quest for goodness – a goodness that one mustn't expect from others, but dispense oneself. Our parents never taught us this.

Since they are marvellous teachers, we try hard to please them and do very well in all subjects. This makes up for the daily grind.

Because we don't have time to go back to Golfe-Juan for lunch and the school on the hill has no canteen, Madame Féraud, the headmistress, has agreed to let us eat lunch in our classroom during the lunchbreak, when all the other students go home to their families. Alone at our desks, we take out our thermoses, lay out our paper plates, unfold the napkins containing our knives and forks. We're ill at ease – afraid of soiling our exercise books, staining the floor, or messing up our clothes. We nibble carefully, avoiding any awkward gestures, with one eye on our thermoses and the other on our metal cups precariously balanced on the slanted desktop. Our gestures are like those of bomb disposal experts defusing a bomb. Sweat trickles down our foreheads.

Often, we limit ourselves to dessert. In our struggle to avoid clumsiness, our best allies are apples, bananas and oranges.

Once we've gobbled down our meal, we go out into the playground and hang about until the school gates reopen for the other students. There we feel free – free to let our imaginations wander.

'Last night, I dreamt I was a bird. I flew over a house.'

'Me too. What was your house like?'

'Very small, with a chimney and a garden full of flowers.'

'What kind of flowers?'

'Stocks, irises, peonies. There was a dog.'

'That's funny, Pablito, I had the very same dream.'

We dream the same, we laugh at the same moments, we have the same enthusiasms and the same feelings, we experience the same confusion. We're identical. We can't live without each other. We're Siamese twins. Nothing will separate us.

We're invited to lunch with Reverend Monod, to whom the school on the hill owes its reputation. 'We' meaning Pablito, me and Mienne, our mother.

Mienne has put her hair up and she is wearing a black outfit that makes her look more virtuous. However her bust is just as provocative and her conversation just as peculiar. For once her favourite subject isn't Picasso but her Protestant family in Lyon.

'A respectable family of researchers, biologists and reputed scientists. Upper-class people who gave me a religious upbringing . . .'

The Reverend and his wife listen to her indulgently.
God will know how to recognize his own.

I remember the Lotte family that my mother painted in
such holy colours for the Reverend's benefit. Among them
there was Renée, my mother's cousin, and her daughter
Christine, a chubby little girl with plaits and pleated skirts.
They used to come on holiday to Golfe-Juan and stay with
my maternal grandmother. In the afternoon they would
join us on the beach where Mienne greeted them over-
exuberantly.

I was ashamed: ashamed of her playacting and ashamed
of our poverty. When they invited us to a restaurant or to
join them on holiday, we had to turn them down because
we wouldn't be able to reciprocate.

They probably thought my mother was stingy. How
could we bear the name Picasso and be penniless at the
same time?

'Quick, Madame! Marina has fainted!'

In a daze, I hear Pablito sobbing and Madame Féraud's
voice in the background: 'Lay her down! Unfasten the
collar of her blouse! Rub her neck!'

These fainting spells – that Madame Féraud called
anxiety attacks – were coming over me more and more
often. There would be a white veil in front of my eyes, a
buzzing in my ears and my forehead would break out into
a sweat. Neither Pablito nor I wanted to tell our mother
about them. We knew what she would say: 'It's your age,'
'You're too self-absorbed,' 'You ate something that didn't
agree with you,' 'You're making my life impossible.'

Nevertheless, she took me to the doctor. When he told
her that I had the first signs of tuberculosis, she conveyed

the news to my father. He didn't believe her. He thought it was a ruse to extract money from him and his father.

Nice 1959. I have become a patient of Doctor Barraya at the Pasteur Hospital. I stay there several times for periods of three weeks to a month. I weigh only thirty kilos and look like a skeleton. I lie on the bed staring at the intravenous solutions dripping slowly into my arm.

One drop, two drops, three drops . . . I must be careful not to move. If the needle slips out of the vein, the nurse will have to insert it again. My arms are covered with bruises.

One drop, two drops, three drops . . . Eighty-seven drops to go and I'll be able to get up and get dressed. Then it will be time for the treatment: two hours of lying looking at the ceiling. After that, it will be lunchtime. Then, it's . . .

Time seems to stand still.

Pablito isn't allowed to visit but one of his drawings is tacked up on the wall above my bed: a woman selling vegetables at the market in Nice. It's the last drawing he'll make. There won't be any others. My mother has harped on about the fact that he has his grandfather's talent so much that she has completely turned him off. He has put his crayons away.

My mother comes to see me. One of her boyfriends has driven her over. She announces that she won't be able to stay for long. She tells me that she's managed to rent out the apartment on the Rue Chabrier. She's found a garden apartment in a villa – the Villa Habana – in Golfe-Juan.

'It's like Picasso's place,' she says. 'You can see the sea from the windows.'

'Can I have a dog?'

'Dogs are expensive. We can't afford it.'

'What about a cat?'

'We'll see.'

Down below, in the car park, someone is honking his horn. She raises her head and says, 'They're waiting for me. I have to go. Be good.'

Not a word from my father. He doesn't once come to see me.

I turn nine.

Shocked that my case is just like that of a child on welfare, Dr Barraya has decided to write my grandfather to tell him that my condition is serious and that I must be sent to the mountains to convalesce. He has already taken the initiative of enrolling me in a children's centre at Villard-de-Lans in the department of Isère. His letter is dry and blunt; it doesn't mince words.

The reply is not immediate. Picasso has other things on his mind. My health can wait.

I complain. I don't want to leave Pablito. I need him and he needs me. If they send me away, I won't let myself be treated, I'll run away, they won't find me.

Dr Barraya tries to calm me down. I refuse to listen. If I'm separated from my brother, I'll let myself die.

What exactly happened? Did Dr Barraya send my grandfather a second letter? Did my father appeal to Picasso? I tend towards another hypothesis: ashamed of being involved in something that might cast him in an unfavourable light, I think my grandfather decided to win double credit and suggest that Pablito go with me to Villard-de-Lans.

The ideal grandfather who pampers his grandchildren — but only for the sake of appearances.

Villard-de-Lans, the pastures, the pure air, the good milk, the bread and butter – and my lungs are healed. Alone with Pablito, who follows me around like a shadow, I feel freer than I've ever felt. After all those years in prison with a self-centred mother, father and grandfather, I feel the need to unburden myself. My victims are the couple that direct the children's centre. I tell them everything: 'My grandfather wanted to send us to the Soviet Union. My mother started a lawsuit against him. My father is afraid of him.'

I'm a gossip. Nothing can stop me. It's like amateur therapy. I pour my heart out to them and tell them all about the fears I've had. Appalled, the directress phones my mother to warn her: 'She should be told not to blab. It could harm Picasso's reputation.'

My mother takes over where I left off. On the subject of Picasso, she's inexhaustible: 'His grandchildren are sacred to him. He wanted to adopt them but I wouldn't let him.'

We return to Golfe-Juan and the Villa Habana. While we've been away, our mother has found a new boyfriend. His name is Jean – a twenty-two-year-old who makes pottery and plastic jewellery. In other words – an artist. My mother works with him. In a shed not far from the house, they mould plastic into pendants, good-luck charms, large panels representing the seabed. They incorporate dried seahorses bought from a retailer. The venture does well. My mother is happy that she's earning enough and doesn't have to badger my father who, of course, always forgets to send us our money by mail. I help out during the summer holidays and earn a bit myself making necklaces with beads and eucalyptus pods. It allows me to contribute my share to the household expenses and feed the two emaciated cats that I've adopted.

Pablito doesn't want me to give them names. All he says is: 'Spare them the grief.'

9

My father has arranged to meet us at La Frégate, a bar in Golfe-Juan. He has recently married Christine Pauplin, whom we know because we spent a holiday with her and my father at Boisgeloup, Picasso's château near Gisors. Picasso bought this property when he was still happily married to my grandmother Olga.

I have only vague recollections of Christine. All I remember is that she was careful not to come between our father and us. She was relaxed, probably out of indifference, and she let my brother and me play with the children from the neighbouring farms who taught us how to chase birds out of copses and with whom we played hide-and-seek in barns and in the ruins of a little ivy-covered chapel on the Boisgeloup estate. We used to collect eggs in the hen-house, milk the cows and drink their frothy milk. I liked the pleasant smell of the stables and the newly cut hay. I enjoyed feeling mud and straw between my fingers, and stroking the backs of heifers and calves. I felt like nothing could make me dirty. It was a serene life and my father was cheerful. He laughed and was amused to see us autonomous, and to be autonomous himself. Grandfather wasn't around to set traps for him.

I don't think Christine ever idealized my father. She accepted him as he was, with his qualities and faults. I don't think she ever tried to seduce Picasso either. She was probably sorry that my father was a slave to him, but she knew she couldn't change anything. She belonged to that category of women who, when they love a man, accept everything about him.

La Frégate. My father is already there. He's smoking a cigarette. In front of him, there's an ashtray full of Gitanes stubs. He clicks his fingers to call the waiter and orders.

'One hot chocolate and one Coke.'

The chocolate is for me, the Coke for Pablito.

'Everything okay at school? You look well . . .'

The usual questions: school, our health, our plans for the week.

We have no plans.

Silence and then he says, 'I haven't had time to see you. I've just got back from Paris. Your grandfather needed brushes and other supplies. He knows he can count on me . . .'

We'd like to talk to him about Bernard, the baby he's had with his new wife. A legitimate child, of Picasso stock like Pablito and me. But we don't dare broach the subject, and nor does he.

He has already stood up to pay the bill. He peels a hundred francs from a wad of notes that he has pulled out of his pocket. He looks surprised that Pablito hasn't touched his Coke.

'You're not going to leave it, are you?' he asks reproachfully.

Pablito raises his glass and drinks it in one go . . . then

heads for the toilet door. When he returns his eyes are red from tears. He went to throw up – not because of the Coke, but because of a father who doesn't know how to love.

The Protestant school has been more concerned with providing its students with a good education than with getting them to pay. As a result, Reverend Monod has warned my mother that the school is about to close due to of lack of funds. We're in despair. What will become of us?

Our mother takes action immediately. In spite of her quarrels with my grandfather, she writes to him explaining that she had managed to place us in a school on her own, but that now she needs his help. He must contribute to our education. She goes to great lengths to appeal to him. She sends another letter to Maître Antébi, my grandfather's lawyer, and asks the headmaster of the Cours Chateaubriand to step in. He writes to Picasso as well, saying he has kept a space for us in his school and is waiting for an answer. It finally arrives: 'Refer to my lawyer.'

'Two erasers ... two rulers ... two compasses ... two books ... two exercise books ...'

Pablito and I choose our school supplies in the small bookshop where arrangements have been made with our grandfather through Maître Antébi. Two erasers, two rulers, two compasses, two books, two exercise books. We're not allowed anything that is not on the list. Everything is totted up. If we need an additional book, we must consult the lawyer. He manages my grandfather's money. His duty is to be vigilant.

The Cours Chateaubriand is a posh establishment; many

of the students are the children of well-to-do families who have been placed there so their parents can deal with their divorce, adultery, stock-market or money problems. Children who are doomed to perpetuate a reputation, a name, and a fortune. Neglected daddy's boys who, while they wait for their turn in the limelight, spend their weekends and often their holidays walled up inside the Cours Chateaubriand. Just like us, they are past masters at the art of hiding their family background. Just like us, they're ashamed of being orphans with famous names. Only the teachers summon us back to reality. The fame that we are supposed to represent is an honour to them. Later, they'll proclaim everywhere, 'I taught history, maths, or French to the little Picasso kids.' No doubt one of the greatest academic distinctions.

No more thermos bottles and veal stew, no more lunches eaten in the classroom like paupers. The Cours Chateaubriand has a real restaurant – not a canteen – with white tablecloths and a feast of good things. We lose our appetite faced with such abundance.

Be that as it may, this week the little Picasso kids couldn't afford the gym outfits that their instructor asked them to buy. The headmaster must wait for Maître Antébi to give his consent, and Maître Antébi must first discuss the matter with their grandfather.

The reply will come two months later.

This week, the little Picasso kids are summoned into the headmaster's office. He informs them that their grandfather still hasn't paid for the past two terms, even though he has been sent several letters to remind him that the tuition fees are past due. Their hearts sinking, the little Picasso kids have to talk to their mother about this.

'This matter doesn't concern me,' she writes to the

director. 'I refer you to Picasso and his administrative staff.'

Two months later, the room and board are paid for the full year. But not the books that we've had to buy since then.

We must start all over again, with new requests. The little Picasso kids are fed up with playing the messenger.

Another spring at Cours Chateaubriand. Pablito and I are now teenagers. After lunch, the students go to the terrace of a brasserie near the school for coffee. We can't go with them. They're wealthy and we're poor. Since there are no classes this afternoon, they'll probably be going to the cinema, or the beach at Cannes. Beach–mats, parasols, pedal–boats, soft drinks . . . They can afford everything with their pocket money.

Pocket money: a word that is not in our personal vocabulary.

Sometimes we get invited to their houses for parties, or on their fathers' boats. We have to prevaricate, make up a story to turn down these invitations that we can't reciprocate: 'We can't go out just like that. We're very protected.'

How can we explain that our mother can't make ends meet, that our father has forgotten to send the infamous allowance, that we're the furthest thing from the mind of the richest painter in the world?

It's true. We're very protected.

Boulevard Carnot, the station, the overheated bus and, at the end of the road, Golfe-Juan: this is our daily life. Occasionally we go to the beach with our local friends. They don't ask questions. They know everything about us. They couldn't care less about Picasso. They're our family.

Freedom and escape were intertwined in my mind. I had

dreams of travelling around the world. The names of some cities were particularly evocative: Singapore, Melbourne, Baghdad, Calcutta. I craved far-away, wide-open spaces.

To indulge this dream, I used to borrow a moped from one of our friends and go off alone along the little coastal roads, with the wind blowing through my hair: Antibes, Cap d'Antibes, La Napoule, Théoule . . . I didn't give a thought to the time, or the danger I was exposed to. The only thing that mattered was the distance separating me from my past. I would stop for a dip in the rocky red inlets of the Estérel. After the swim, I would eat a tomato and a piece of bread that I'd brought with me. I was living an itinerant, adventurous life. I was a nomad.

Once, the police stopped me on the road into Saint-Tropez. I had no identification papers on me and refused to tell them my name. They let me go because I was nice and I looked happy.

When I didn't have a moped, my friends and I used to hitchhike: 'We've missed the bus. Could you drop us off at Juan-les-Pins?'

It always worked. The angelic smile, the innocent look, and we would embark for the enchanted isle of Cythera in unfamiliar cars.

The Cours Chateaubriand closes its doors for the summer holidays and the students stand in front of the school entrance talking about their plans.

'Where are you going this year? To the West Indies?'

'No, I'm going to join my mother in Miami. After that, I don't know. I'll probably go to my father's in Ireland. He just remarried.'

Now they turn to us: 'Of course, you'll be going to Spain with your grandfather?'

'Yes, of course.'

'Yes of course.'

Once again, we're playing the game of being the lucky kids that Picasso dotes on.

A visit to Notre-Dame-de-Vie. Our father has picked us up at the Cannes–Vallauris crossroads.

'Get in quick,' he says through the wound-down window of his car. 'We're late.'

Late for the divine audience that grandfather is graciously granting to his son and grandchildren.

The gate to Notre-Dame-de-Vie is hermetically sealed. My father rings the bell: two short rings, one long one. We hear Jacqueline's voice on the intercom.

'Who is it?'

She knows it's our father and that he's with us. He's the only person to ring the bell this way to signal his arrival. However, she wants to let us know, even before we enter, that we're undesirables. She wants to humiliate us. Monseigneur is hers and hers alone. No one has the right to trespass and destroy the web she's spun around her lord and master.

'Who is it?'

She doesn't give up. She wants an answer.

'It's Paulo.'

The electric lock clicks open aggressively – like a reproach. The Afghan hounds immediately growl at us, their teeth barred. They are the fierce watchdogs of the realm of darkness which we are entering and they follow us around diligently. They would like nothing better than to jump on us.

Unhurriedly, we walk up the gravel path edged with cypress trees and boxwood. Jacqueline is waiting for us at the threshold of the house, with its cold and austere walls. She is wearing black. Her waist has filled out and her face is drawn.

'Monseigneur is in the small drawing room,' she says to my father. 'He was going to take a nap.'

In other words: 'Don't linger.'

Grandfather greets us sitting in an armchair. On the table in front of him is a steaming cup and a bottle containing drops that Jacqueline has asked him to take. Our father told us in the car driving over that, for some time now, his father has been very worried about his health. In fact, no one is fooled. Everyone knows that he isn't sick and never has been. His doctor – who was also Matisse's – only comes for form's sake. He knows that his patient's ailments are due to his fear of ageing.

One thing reassures Picasso, however. All his friends have died and he's still around. All of them: Cocteau, Matisse, Braque, André Breton, Derain, Paul Eluard, his communist comrade, and Sabartès, his faithful companion and cohort at Els Quatre Gats, the Catalan café that, in 1900, hosted the first one-man show of a young painter by the name of Pablo Ruiz y Picasso.

As well as all the others who were his intimate friends and whom he rejected because he stopped liking them – arbitary slaughter.

Grandfather is immortal. Pablito and I know this. He is the strongest man in the world. He has all the power. He can't die.

We walk up to him shyly in the large vaulted room where he receives the few people who are still admitted to Notre-Dame-de-Vie. He stares at us with his phosphorous gaze from behind the corrective glasses he has recently started wearing. He hardly smiles at us.

'So how's school?' he asks Pablito.

And then he adds as an afterthought, 'And how's your mother, Marina?'

We just nod. What answers can we give to such questions?

'Are you going away on holiday?' he asks without even looking at us.

'No,' Pablito replies in a choked voice.

'That's good . . . that's good,' he answers evasively.

What does he care about our holidays? Or our studies? He isn't interested in anything outside of himself.

Jacqueline comes into the room like a shadow. She walks up to my father and whispers in his ear. My father nods with a pained look and turns toward us.

'Marina, Pablito,' he says in a pathetic voice, 'it's time to go. Pablo needs to be alone. You've made him tired.'

We've made him tired though he hasn't bestowed one second of attention on us.

Jacqueline leaves us at the entrance steps. She shakes hands with us grudgingly and immediately goes back to join her Sun. 'I'm coming . . . I'm coming,' she squeals as she rushes into the shuttered house. 'I'm coming, Monseigneur!'

She can't bear the idea of abandoning her executioner for even a second. Without him, she can't breathe, she is a fish out of water.

My grandfather never had time to think about the fate of those close to him. The only thing he cared about was his painting, the suffering and happiness that painting provided. He would do anything to serve it, master it and then disobey it. Just as he crushed tubes of paint to extract the emotion of a colour, he didn't hesitate to crush those who pined for a glance from him. He loved children for their innocence, and women for the sexual, carnivorous impulses they aroused in him. They had to give up their mystery. Mixing blood and sperm, he exalted them in his paintings, imposed his violence on them, and sentenced them to death when he felt a dulling of the sexual power they instilled in him. The voluptuousness he derived from sex and from painting was of the same essence. Through both, he tried to resolve his passion and contempt for women. He saw them as harbingers of death. Monarch of the realm of darkness, he worked on them at night in his studio. They had to be present, subservient and obedient. He taunted them with his paintbrush to the point of exhaustion: *Verónicas* in blue and orange; *Faenas* in fiery reds, crimsons and blacks. They were his prey. He was the Minotaur. These were bloody, indecent bullfights from which he always emerged the dazzling winner.

Anything outside this malevolent alchemy did not interest him. All those who escaped or were no longer an object of his gluttony left him cold. They lay in a cemetery of oblivion, with no cross or recognition, no gratitude or compassion. Whether they were women, friends, children or grandchildren, his victims had to be sacrificed to his art.

He was Picasso. He was a genius.

A genius shows no mercy. His glory depends on it.

10

I decide I will have nothing more to do with this wretchedness. I've had enough of violence, weakness, the control of a despot over my life and Pablito's. I want my freedom, my own breathing space. I want to extricate myself from this family.

'Pablito, we must work.'

'What for? You know we'll never break away. We're Picassos.'

In short, we're doomed to suffer.

I've decided that I won't suffer any more. I will defy my fate.

In the summer, there are many outdoor day camps on the Côte d'Azur for the children of working parents. I note down their addresses and send them my CV. 'Studying for the Baccalaureate, serious and conscientious, seeking job as a supervisor.' I receive answers and go for interview.

'Your name?'

'Marina Ruiz Picasso.'

'The daughter?'

'No, the granddaughter.'

'Oh, the granddaughter!'

How do I look to these people? Like a difficult child who wants to work just to stand up to her family? A rich kid who wants to take food away from the poor? Looking for work when your name is Picasso? What nerve! What contempt for others!

What can I do but tell the truth? I stutter, 'I love children and later, if I study medicine, I'd like to specialize in paediatrics. If you take me and trust me, I'll make myself as useful as I can.'

Always beating around the bush, trying to erase the Picasso stamp, always having to turn the other cheek when confronted with sarcastic remarks, accepting any lousy job and, above all, going to great lengths to be liked. Not by the people in charge who have accepted me on a trial basis, but by the children. I win them over and they tell me their dreams: 'Later, I'll take mummy on a trip around the world. We'll never leave each other.' 'Later, I'll drive a train, like my dad.'

These 'laters' are full of hope. They make my heart bleed.

The summer before my Baccalaureate exams, things are different. Instead of working in a holiday camp, I get a temporary job in the Golfe-Juan Post Office. I deliver telegrams to residents and holiday-makers – a job that fills me with enormous pride.

'Do you have a way of getting around?' asks the postmaster when I introduce myself.

'Of course.'

I'm lying, but I have no choice. I must get this job, particularly since the postmaster has also agreed to hire Pablito to sort the mail – for this is the season when the mail arrives in overflowing sacks. I run to a bicycle shop and explain my problem. The proprietor agrees to sell me a second-hand moped on credit, with the first payment at the end of June and the final payment in early October. And at no extra cost, he will check the brakes, replace the cylinders in the engine and straighten out the front mudguard. It's a deal! I can finally call myself a telegram delivery girl, and Pablito a sorting clerk and co-owner of a used moped.

With a mailbag slung over my shoulder, I tour the streets, ringing bells at garden gates and buzzing the intercoms of blocks of flats.

'Telegram for you!'

In the holiday season, there are very few telegrams that bring bad tidings. Usually they announce the arrival of a relative, the birth of a child, some happy event . . . and they fetch me a tip that will allow me to get new tyres for Pegasus, our moped.

Pablito is happy as well. He's the fastest at sorting letters. He feels competent. He has colour in his cheeks.

Every week, we give our entire salary to our mother. We consider this normal. We must stick together.

I don't recall ever buying clothes without telling her. My tailor and Pablito's was the Prisunic supermarket. A skirt from its shelves, a cotton blouse, a T-shirt, a pair of canvas trousers was all we needed for the summer. We took good care of these clothes. They had to last until the beginning of school.

Sunday was a gloomy day. The beach packed with bathers, the café terraces with their hoards of tourists depressed us. Having neither the means nor the desire to mingle with this crowd, we would stay in our room until Monday morning. Since our father made no effort to see us, we were cut off from our grandfather who would be eighty-seven in October. Pablito had tried telephoning him but had got Jacqueline

'Who are you?'

'His grandson.'

'Who?'

'I'd like to speak to my grandfather.'

'But who are you?'

'Pablo.'

'Pablo? There's only one Pablo, young man. And that Pablo can't see you.'

She might just as well have plunged a knife into my brother's heart: it was a sacrilege for him to bear the name he'd been given; he was a contemptible usurper.

And Jacqueline added in her sour, disdainful voice, 'The Maître isn't home, but you can write to him.'

I shed many tears during my analysis recalling the letters that Pablito and I wrote to a grandfather who never bothered to answer them. Letters that Jacqueline probably tore up. Letters that grandfather never even opened. Letters in which we tried to tell him that we were capable of loving, helping and understanding him.

Letters that we didn't send.

Letters that said essentially, 'We're your grandchildren and we need you. We don't want to be little visiting monkeys hiding behind a father for whom you have contempt. We want to see you alone and find out what is on your mind. We want you to tell us about your childhood in Malaga, about Don José Ruiz, your father, and Doña María Picasso López, your mother, whose name, size and eyes you inherited. We want to hear about your little sister Lola. And your uncle Salvador who, when you were born, blew smoke from his cigar into your nose to revive you when the midwife thought you were dead. And Maria de los Remedios, your godmother, who breastfed you because your mother, Doña Maria, was too exhausted . . . You see, since you have stolen our father, we must appeal to you for our genealogical tree, our backbone. To construct the present, we need a past. Help us, Grandfather. For once, please help us.'

October. School starts again at the Cours Chateaubriand. It's the last year of school for both Pabilto and me. We have been in the same year since primary school, when Pabilto deliberately did badly so he would have to repeat a year and could be in the same class as me. We always did everything we could to be together and now we're both studying philosophy, reappraising things in the light of Gide, Nietzsche, Proust, Rimbaud and Stendhal. We and the other students vie with one another about what we know and how we feel. We tear one another apart over a thought, an idea, or an ideology.

We investigate the human soul, go into ecstasies over an aphorism; argue, quibble, burn, swoon. With theses and antitheses, we assert our personalities.

In the course of these verbal sparring matches, the boys and girls try to seduce each other with a glance or a smile. Couples are formed in response to a sentence by Camus, or a line by Prévert.

I liked these discreet, self-conscious courtships. I was attracted to the attentive, gallant, romantic boys who self-effacingly opened doors for me, controlled their ardour, and behaved courteously. Fingers touching lightly, or a kiss on the cheek were enough to set my heart pounding. The only thing I demanded was that they respect me, that Pablito like them and that they like Pablito.

I was starry-eyed and, when one of them gave me a cheap ring he had won at a fair, I began to daydream wildly. I was so attached to symbolic gestures that the ring fired my imagination. I would finally be able to erase the hot-iron brand of Picasso.

I was gullible then.

Pablito had a crush on a girl in our class. Her name was Dominique and she was Corsican. She was pretty, gentle and thoughtful.

Pablito wanted to tell her of his love. But how do you say 'I love you' when there has never been love in your childhood? Being a discreet and secretive person, he didn't dare speak to his young Corsican. He tried to communicate with her in looks.

But Dominique didn't notice Pablito's glances. How could she know that Pablito was attracted to her if he didn't speak up?

'What should I do?' he asked me one evening in our room.

'Do you want me to talk to her?'

'I have so many things to tell her.'

'You should write to her.'

Words are unruly things. Pablito kept putting off his letter; he couldn't seem to express his feelings. He was too anxious, too wounded, too many of his hopes had been smashed.

In the end Pablito procrastinated for too long. Dominique found someone else.

My father telephones the school. He wants to see us, but Pablito refuses — he doesn't want to suffer anymore.

I go alone to meet him on the terrace of a café across the street from the train station in Cannes. He's with a young woman whom he's brought back from Paris. Céline – that's her name – must be nineteen. Nearly the same age as me. He whispers into my ear, 'Céline is just a friend. Nothing more than a friend.'

From my amused look, he understands that I don't believe a word. Whether Céline is a friend or girlfriend, he doesn't need to worry. I certainly won't mention her to my mother, or to Christine if I happen to run into her. His playboy attitude has long since ceased to appall me. In a way, he's a stranger to me.

'Your brother didn't want to come?' he asks in a pitiful voice.

'He couldn't.'

No more words are exchanged. We have so few things to say to each other . . . and are so inhibited.

Fortunately, Céline is here, with her affected mannerisms, her little laugh, her fluttering eyelashes. She's proud of being with the son and granddaughter of Picasso, the super-famous painter. She feels like a celebrity.

We have moved from the Villa Habana to the Villa La Rémajo, a new house my mother has found in the hills above Golfe-Juan. It has a garden full of flowers, and a view of pink sunsets over the sea and the Estérel mountains.

We're only a few months away from the Baccalaureate exams. Pablito is sitting cross-legged on his bed. His lips quiver as he murmurs some lines of Baudelaire:

> *The Devil stirs about me without rest,*
> *And round me floats like noxious air and thin*
> *I breathe this poison-air which scalds my breast*

1917. Olga Kokhlova as a ballerina in Diaghilev's Ballets Russes. This was the year she met Picasso. They would marry one year later.

Summer, 1921. Olga in Picasso's garage studio at Fontainebleau, surrounded by pastel sketches of her for the painting 'Three Women at a Fountain' (1921).

Antibes, summer 1923.
Picasso and Paulo on the
beach at La Garoupe.

Antibes, summer 1923.
Picasso, Olga and Paulo
on the beach at La Garoupe.

Normandy, summer 1925. Paulo Picasso (born 24 February, 1921).
The photograph recalls the painting 'Paulo on a Donkey' (1923).

Cannes, 1957. Picasso and Paulo at La Californie, which now belongs to Marina.

A New Year greetings card made by Olga in 1951.
This page: (top) Pablito's birthday; (bottom) Pablo surrounded by the
Ruiz y Picasso family in Barcelona in the 1930s.

This page: (clockwise from top left) Olga on her wedding day, Marina as a baby, Pablo holding Paulo, Paulo and his dog, Pablo and Olga in 1921; (centre) Paulo. (The three babies in the small photos have not been identified).

Circa 1951. Picasso with Marina (born 14 November, 1950).

Paulo holding Pablito (born 5 May, 1949) and Marina.

(*Opposite page*) Vallauris, 1956. A party at Picasso's house La Galloise. Marina and Pablito are in the foreground. Picasso is with Jean Cocteau. It was with Cocteau that Picasso went to Rome in 1917 to work on the scenery for *Parade*. There he met Olga, his future wife.

© André Villers

Vallauris, 1954.
Pablito.

1954. Paulo with
Pablito and Marina.

© André Villers

Normandy, *circa* 1957. Marina and Pablito on the Boisgeloup estate.

Normandy, *circa* 1957. Paulo with Marina and Pablito at Boisgeloup.

(*Opposite page*)
Golfe-Juan, summer 1956.
Emilienne Lotte with Pablito
and Marina.

Villard-de-Lans.
Marina and Pablito.

Vauvenargues.
Marina and Pablito in front of Picasso's bronze, 'Man with Sheep' (1943).

Circa 1968.
Pablito.

1970. Pablito with Lassy the dog.

'The Village of Youth', founded by Marina in 1990 and situated in Thu Doc, a northern suburb of Ho Chi Minh City. It consists of a school, a gymnasium, a swimming pool, a park and a number of small houses designed to create a family atmosphere.

1997. Marina on a visit to one of the orphanages financed by her foundation.

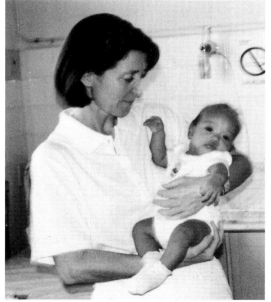

1997. Marina on a visit to one of the day-nurseries supported by her foundation.

Thu Duc, 1992. Marina at the Village of Youth with her children Gaël and Flore, and a child from the foundation.

1992. Marina holding a child
from Go Vap, an orphanage
refurbished by her foundation.

Thu Duc, 1992. Marina in front of one of the family houses at the
Village of Youth with the two 'mothers'.

Cannes, 2001. Marina at La Californie, in front of a portrait of her grandmother ('Portrait of Olga', 1923).

Baudelaire, Rimbaud, Chénier, Verlaine, Apollinaire . . . He is thirsty for poems that glorify suffering, despair and death. His studies no longer interest him.

'What for?' he keeps repeating. 'I have no future.'

I lose my temper, reprimand him, and try to reason with him: 'Come on, pull yourself together. Everyone has a place on earth.'

He shrugs his shoulders. I annoy him. He becomes aggressive: 'Stop lecturing me and leave me alone. Why hide from it? We're caught in a trap from which we'll never escape.'

His eyes are blazing. He gets up, shouting at me as he walks out of the room, 'I leave you to your illusions! They might cost you a lot.'

He was right. They have cost me a lot.

Pablito has left a note on the living-room table: 'I won't be back tonight.'

My mother is extremely upset.

'Did he tell you where he was going? Why is he doing this to me?'

I don't say a word. I'm determined not to feed her fears. I'm all too aware of what her anxiety will lead to: shouts, moans, shortness of breath, blackouts, emergency calls to a doctor. High drama. A drama I reject.

'Pablito will be back. He must have gone to see a friend.'

'After everything I have done for him!'

A narcissistic outburst. Persecution mania. As always, depicting herself as a victim.

'Calm down, Pablito will be back.'

No sign of Pablito at the Cours Chateaubriand. Where is he? No one knows and I'm worried. He's been gone for three days now. No news. I make endless tours of the roads around Golfe-Juan, Vallauris and Valbonne on my moped. I shout his name into the scrubland, the woods and the ravines.

The only answer I get is an echo.

When, on the fourth day, Pablito still doesn't show up, the headmaster sends a letter to Maître Antébi, the only relay between my father and us. My father, who has been notified by Maître Antébi, summons me.

'Your brother has been cutting classes for three days. If you see him, tell him I don't want any trouble. Your grandfather has sacrificed enough for him. His schooling is expensive. He could at least show some gratitude.'

He doesn't think of asking why Pablito is acting this way. For him, it's childishness, childishness that might tarnish his relationship with his own father. And earn him the inevitable criticism: 'You're a good for nothing!'

Pablito came back as he always did when he ran away. But he ran away more and more often. Where did he go? I had no idea. He refused to tell me and I respected his silence.

Much later – alas much too late – my analysis helped me understand that he must have lost all hope. Unable to put his suffering into words, he needed another form of escape: walking uninterruptedly for miles through open spaces, sleeping in the hollow of a rock, choosing roads at random helped him to shake off the burden of reality. He sought the void. He desperately desired an undefineable 'elsewhere.'

He would come back without a word, worn out, his cheeks drawn. From a twig stuck to his sweater you could tell that he had lain down in a field; from sand in his shoes, that he had walked and maybe slept on the beach. Had he even thought of eating? Out of respect, I didn't question him. He was in his own world.

— 11 —

We take the Baccalaureate exam and get the results. Pablito and I pass. What a relief! Given the chaos in our life, passing was unexpected.

In front of the gates of the Cours Chateaubriand students stand around talking about their future plans.

'My parents have advised me to do the exams for the Institute of Political Science or business school. Later, I'll be taking over the family business . . .'

'I've decided to go to law school. Afterwards I'll be working in my father's law firm . . .'

I know what I want to do. I want to go to medical school and become a paediatrician.

My mother suggests I discuss it with Maître Antébi. He raises his arms in the air: 'Medical school! That's seven years of study! Did you think about the cost? Your grandfather will never agree.'

It's true, let's not daydream. Not only will Picasso refuse to help me, I can already guess what he'll say: 'Did I study anything? You'd be better off as a waitress in a bar.'

A waitress in a bar. True, I could go to medical school and pay for my studies by working at night as a dishwasher in a bar. Many people have done that. But the difference between these 'many' and me is that I have not been brought up in a loving household and I don't have the stability that would give me the strength to be a dishwasher or cleaner whilst doing my studies. How can you aspire to a place in the sun when you've always lived in the shadow of unhappiness?

Pablito has also understood that nothing will come his way. A fatalist, he accepts defeat. But can it even be called defeat when you don't fight any more? When you have no desire to fight any more?

Yet for a long time he had dreams of writing. Writing to try to communicate; writing for the sake of writing. He wanted to leave for Africa and describe the animals; travel to a glacier and witness the melting of the snows; hide himself away and record the things that moved and fascinated him.

But you can't make a living that way. To make a living entails fighting. Not for Pablito, who has given up, but for me who is still alive. With my experience looking after children, I find a job in a hospice at Vallauris, in the unit for the seriously handicapped. I take care of a group of autistic, psychotic, schizophrenic and severely retarded children. I get them up, wash and dress them, make them eat, keep them busy, and work with a psychologist who comes twice a week. The children are quite a group. Some chew their fingers; some howl all day; others remain prostrated, while others walk tirelessly around their room. The most aggressive ones have to be tied down when they go to sleep. They hit me, or throw plates of pasta in my face. I don't scold them; I refuse to do what some orderlies do and tie them up to make them eat. I wash the hands of the ones who eat their excrement; I make them brush their teeth; I caress their heads.

The smell of that excrement will cling to my skin and soul for many years; the smell of misery, misfortune and malediction.

The nurses, the cleaners, the cooks and the orderlies – they've all learned that I'm Picasso's granddaughter.

'She's sneering at us. What's she doing here?'

The more malicious give me the most demeaning tasks. The union activists want me to join: 'With your name on the list, we'll have more clout.'

After analysis, the paths one has chosen in life cease to be impenetrable. I didn't choose this kind of work by chance. It was not by chance that later I went to Vietnam to help children in distress. I worked in the Vallauris hospice so I would feel less lonely. Unconsciously, I needed to empathize with the misfortune of those handicapped children so I could cope with my own misfortune. It brought my own life into perspective.

They didn't cling to me; I clung to them.

As a favour to Comrade Picasso, the communist town council of Vallauris said that Pablito could be librarian at a trauma unit for car accident victims: amputees who needed physical therapy; people who were half or completely paralysed. Pablito seemed content with this. Books were his passion.

Alas, the position he was promised was not free. In the meantime, the head of personnel offered him a job as an orderly – emptying the chamberpots, sweeping the floor, changing the patients' soiled sheets . . .

Pablito accepted. After all, he had accepted everything for so long, especially the unacceptable.

My mother inspects me from head to foot.

'You could do something about your appearance,' she says. 'With a face like yours you should use make up. And look at your hair! And your dress. You look like a tramp.'

Disgusted, she adds, 'It's true, you can't wear the same kind of clothes as me. You don't have my bust. Or my legs. Life hasn't been that kind to you.'

I don't answer. I'm too tired.

Pablito is already asleep when I go to join him in our room. A collection of Rimbaud's poetry is lying on his chest. I open it at the book mark and read the lines that he has underlined with a rapid pencil mark:

> *Perfumes don't make his nostrils quiver;*
> *He sleeps in the sun, his hand on his chest*
> *Quietly. There are two red holes in his right side . . .*

Pablito is smiling in his sleep.

The days go by; each day like the next. The ring of the alarm clock, tea with no sugar, a shower and the journey to work.

My mother doesn't have a boyfriend any more and is dependent on her few friends to get around, so I buy a little VW. 'Economical, solid, and never breaks down,' says the brochure I find in our mailbox. After much bargaining, the Volkswagon dealer agrees to let me pay for it over five years.

'Only because it's you!'

For once the Picasso name helps me: I get credit – a quarter of my salary every month.

My mother is delighted with my acquisition.

'Marina, when you leave work remember to pick up the bag of shopping I left at the grocer's.'

'Marina, since you've got wheels, stop by the pharmacy and don't forget to get my medical form stamped.'

'Marina, don't forget, you have to drive me to the lab for my medical tests.'

I'm her errand boy, her chauffeur, her servant. She doesn't care that I'm dead tired after work; I'm here to serve her.

My father only wants to see me so he can talk about Picasso.

'Jacqueline has had a lift installed for him at Notre-Dame-de-Vie. He's having more and more trouble getting about. He refuses to see me. What do you think of that, Marina?'

He doesn't ask a single question about what I'm up to. All he says is, 'I hope your grandfather is well. Call me if you have news.'

Pablito is increasingly taciturn. I am now the only person with whom he is willing to communicate.

'So you remember the afternoons we used to spend with our grandmother Olga?'

'Yes, of course, Pablito.'

'Remember the stories she used to tell us in her mother tongue?'

'She loved us, Pablito.'

'I wish I were with her.'

Sunday, 8 April 1973. As always on a Sunday, I'm on duty at the Vallauris hospice. Apart from a few children yelling in their rooms, the place is relatively quiet. The nurse who is taking over the next shift has just arrived. My day is over. I can leave.

Pablito is at the entrance to the building. He has come on his moped. He rushes up to me and cries in a broken voice, 'Grandfather . . . grandfather. He's dead.'

Grandfather, dead? I can't believe it.

'It's not true, Pablito? How do you know?'

'I heard it on the radio. He died this morning at eleven forty. A heart attack.'

He catches his breath and adds, overcome, 'A heart attack following a pulmonary oedema. That's what they said.'

I'm shattered. Grandfather has died without our seeing him again. Alone with Jacqueline at Notre-Dame-de-Vie, his fortress.

In complete solitude.

On television we watch the stampede of journalists towards the gates of Notre-Dame-de-Vie and listen to the voice-over.

'Yesterday, we were told by his secretary Miguel, Picasso still took his walk through the grounds on the arm of Jacqueline Picasso. She has refused to talk to us. She is overwhelmed with grief. The family doctor is watching over her health.'

We must talk to our father. Pablito telephones Paris. A voice answers that our father has left for the Côte d'Azur.

For the Côte d'Azur, but where on the Côte d'Azur?

Pablito calls the hotels where our father usually stays. On the fourth call, the receptionist tells him that Paulo has just left for Notre-Dame-de-Vie.

'Try calling this evening.'

We have no luck in the evening. On the following day, our father answers and says to Pablito, 'The funeral is tomorrow in the strictest privacy. Jacqueline has asked that no one attend. I'll call you back.'

Pablito is indignant. He is on the verge of tears.

'Even if I must lay siege, I will see my grandfather. I have the right to. No one can take it away from me.'

I try to calm him down.

'Pablito, we haven't been allowed to see him for such a long time. It's useless.'

In spite of my advice, that very afternoon Pablito jumps on his moped and goes to Notre-Dame-de-Vie. He rings the bell at the gate. No one answers. He keeps ringing. A guard suddenly appears with the two Afghans at his side.

'Go away!' he shouts. 'You can't come in. I have orders from Madame Picasso.'

Pablito is obstinate.

'I order you to open the gate. Tomorrow my grandfather is being buried. I want to say goodbye to him.'

'Clear off!' shouts the warder. 'Get out of sight or I'll release the dogs!'

He runs out of the gates, grabs Pablito's moped and throws it into a ditch.

Behind the fence, the dogs are growling.

Inside Notre-Dame-de-Vie, Picasso is lying in his coffin covered by an embroidered black Spanish cape. Jacqueline and my father are by his side.

They haven't heard a thing.

Prostrate in our room, Pablito refuses to speak, eat or see us for two days. I spend the night on the living-room sofa so he can be alone. For once, my mother behaves discreetly. She's careful not to show it, but I think that my grandfather's death is an enormous weight off her mind. She will no longer suffer and, above all, we will no longer suffer.

'What's the point of getting into such a state?' she whispers to me.

A state for which she is partly responsible and accountable.

Alain, our lifelong friend, who, in happier times helped us fix up the dinghy, comes over. Timidly, he pops his head into Pablito's room.

'Are you okay?'

'Yes,' my brother replies.

'Do you want to talk?'

'No, I prefer to rest. I need sleep.'

My mother goes to bed. Before leaving us, she whispers, 'Don't forget, tomorrow you have to pick me up at the hospital where I have to go for tests.'

Endless tests from which she'll come out satisfied and cured. Until the next time.

My night is full of nightmares, of grandfather and his eyes. Flashing, inhuman, like those of a bird of prey. Those blazing, hostile, merciless pupils. And that laugh – enormous, sardonic, cruel.

I wake up with a start, dripping with sweat.

In his room, Pablito is fast asleep. He has left the bedside lamp on.

Thursday, 12 April, nine o'clock. Picasso has been dead for four days. My brother seems calm.

'Did you sleep well, Pablito?'

'Very well,' he replies, in a choked voice.

'I'm going to pick up Mienne at the hospital. Do you need anything?'

'Everything's fine, Marina.'

I'm driving the car. Mienne is next to me. She senses that I don't feel like talking. Talk about what? Her blood pressure? Her cholesterol?

La Fontonne, Antibes, Juan-les-Pins, Golfe-Juan, Avenue Juliette-Adam, the Chemin de la Rampe and, at the very end, the Villa La Rémajo where Pablito must be waiting for us. Eager to get back to him, I drive with the accelerator flat against the floor, cursing the red lights and all the cars that are slowing up traffic because of the Cannes Festival.

I open the door. The cats slip out between my legs, their fur bristling. I have a sudden premonition and I run into the living room. Pablito is lying on the sofa. There is blood on his hair – his hair, his face, his chest. I rush over to him. Blood bubbles from his mouth. And there's a suffocating, horrible, toxic smell, the smell of a hospital or a morgue.

'Pablito! Talk to me!'

He groans. He is breathing.

My mother is panic-stricken. Her distress is so great that she can't utter a word or a cry. She is holding a crumpled little plastic bag that once contained a dose of bleach.

The smell, the bleeding, the foam on his lips . . . Pablito has emptied it.

Fast. We must act fast. I call the emergency services. My God, please make them hurry. I look at my watch. It is eleven thirty. I must be strong. I must not fall apart.

Finally they come with their stretcher. They put Pablito into the red ambulance. I climb up next to him and hold his hand.

'Pablito, it's your little sister!'

A stream comes out of his mouth. All his blood is flowing out of him.

The siren howls wildly. We bump up and down the pavement as the driver weaves through the traffic. Racing against time; racing against death.

Antibes. The emergency unit at the La Fontonne Hospital where I came this morning to pick up my mother.

We are separated. The glass door closes in front of me.

'Hang in there! Don't give up, Pablito!'

The wait. My head is empty from too much suffering, too much anger, too much fear.

Finally, a doctor comes up to me.

'We can't tell yet. We must wait forty-eight hours.'

'Don't give up, Pablito!'

The resuscitation unit. Pablito lies inert on his bed. He breathes jerkily through tubes in his mouth. His irregular heartbeats are monitored on a screen. A machine checks his blood pressure. A tangle of drips connects him to life. His hand inside mine is so soft. So soft and fragile.

The resuscitation unit and now, after so many weeks, the intensive care unit. Pabilto has undergone a whole series of operations on his oesophagus, his stomach and his intestines, all severely damaged by the bleach he drank. He is being fed intravenously. The doctors consider grafts or transplants, but with very little conviction. Then they give up on the idea. The lesions are too serious and it is the kind of surgery for which he would have to be transferred to a state-of-the-art unit in Marseilles or Paris. Where would we find the money for this transfer that could save his life? My father or Jacqueline, as heirs of my grandfather, could easily get the money at a bank, but they don't come forward. Picasso's death has locked them into a nebulous, unhealthy world of their own. They have lost their base, lost their master. Pablito's suicide doesn't count for them. They are floundering in their self-centredness.

Pablito can finally speak. He can finally answer my questions.

'Why did you do this?'

'There was no hope. No other way out.'

'Pablito, we're young. We could find a way out if you would trust me.'

He has the courage to smile.

'Well, you see, I wanted to find a way out, but I didn't succeed.'

'I'm here, Pablito. You can count on me.'

He looks at me and doesn't answer right away. When he finally does speak, his words are heart-rending:

'They didn't want us at his funeral. They didn't want us to be part of their lives. We've never been able to rely on our father, who has never grown up. Now that grandfather is dead, he's in thrall to Jacqueline. Cowardliness and baseness. The Picasso empire refused to let you study medicine. The Picasso empire let you to take that wretched job. The Picasso empire closed all doors to you. These things had to stop. So, you know what, Marina?'

I listen silently.

'I ran away for the last time. To save you, I ran away. I had to do it. A gesture that could match theirs.'

'Please, Pablito!'

'I wanted to implode, destroy all our suffering from the inside. Now, they'll realize that you exist. From now on, they'll take care of you. At least for the sake of public opinion.'

Public opinion – that is to say, the press – pounced on 'the suicide of the century'. Everything that related to Picasso stirred up the journalists.

The famous painter's grandson did not want to live after the death of his grandfather. He was twenty-four years old.

In the shadow of Picasso, his grandson Pablito lived in poverty.

On the lookout for scandal, the journalists rummaged through our private life, questioning everyone who had known us and wallowing in gossip. They described our living conditions in great detail, exploiting and exaggerating things. They turned us into victims and scapegoats.

A few hundred metres away from their grandfather's sumptuous villa, they lived in a state of destitution.

My mother may have played a part in this gossip. I don't know and I don't want to know.

All I cared about was my brother.

There was no sign of life from Maya, Claude, Paloma, or my father. Were they ashamed, or did they fear the revelations of the press? Why didn't they put in an appearance? Was despair contagious?

Marie-Thérèse Walter was the only one to show us kindness and generosity. She came to see my mother and offered to sell two Picasso paintings she owned.

My grandfather's death meant she had no money since she would no longer receive the meagre allowance that he used to give her. Yet she sold those paintings to help us during Pablito's three-month hospital stay – a gesture of great humanity for which I am immensely grateful. Even though I was able to pay her back later on, when I became an heiress, I applaud her goodness and courage.

Her playfulness too, demonstrated in the letter she later sent, which said, 'Now that you are free and ask me what would make me happy in exchange for what I did for you and Pablito, buy me a helicopter.'

I like to think this helicopter was a witticism. Or a show of modesty. Extreme modesty.

After a month and a half, my father finally shows up at the hospital. A nurse tells me that he's waiting outside the ward.

'Pablito, he'd like to see you.'

Pablito turns his head towards me. Speaking exhausts him. I lean over him and repeat, 'Pablito, he'd like to see you.' He smiles sadly and whispers, 'Tell him it's too late. I have nothing to say to him.'

Pablito now weighs only twenty-eight kilos. He will never regain his digestive functions. He is condemned to the life of a disabled person. In spite of that, we make plans:

'You'll see, we'll never leave each other.'

'Will I write?'

'Yes, Pablito, you will.'

'Tell me what it will be like.'

'We'll find a house for the two of us. You'll have your room and I'll have mine. We'll buy curtains for the windows. You'll have a desk, and a typewriter.'

I depict a sunny future so that he will believe in life and forget his suffering.

Wednesday, 11 July. Pablito has been moved into a room upstairs. The doctors have removed his drips. I know what this means. There is no more hope. I must not cry; I must try to smile.

'You know, Marina, I'm beginning to feel well. I'm no longer in pain.'

He doesn't know that he's being given morphine.

'Rest, Pablito. Soon you'll be well. I have to go now. I'll be back tomorrow.'

I must leave this room and speak to a doctor. I want the truth. No matter what it is, I want the truth. From the sombre look of the intern on duty, I understand that my brother is doomed. I don't want to believe it. It seems too unjust.

'He's not going to die, is he?'

'Go home,' he says to me, in a soothing voice. 'If something happens, I promise to call you.'

Curled up in an armchair, I await daybreak. My mother, drained by sorrow, has gone to bed. I look at my watch. It is a quarter to four. Every second counts. Tomorrow. If only tomorrow would come. Four o'clock. The telephone rings. The dreaded telephone. I pick it up, shaking.

'It's over. Your brother has passed away.'

It is 12 July. After a three-month ordeal, Pablito has breathed his last. He is dead.

The press goes wild. On the radio, on television, in the magazines, all they talk about is my brother's death. Or rather the death of 'Picasso's grandson.'

'His name was Pablo, like his grandfather . . .'

He is finally entitled to his name.

Still no news from my father though he has obviously learned of his son's death. How could he not know, given the journalists' uproar over his suicide? I no longer want to see him but I need him, or rather I need his consent so Pablito can be laid to rest next to his grandmother. Maître Ferreboeuf, a young lawyer in Antibes, accepts to write him. For free, of course – how else? For once, my father replies immediately:

'I see no objection.'

We must still find the money to pay for the funeral. I'm in despair. We don't have a penny.

In Cannes, the students on the café terraces whisper among themselves. Discreetly, they each take a note out of their pocket and hand it to one of their school mates. At another table a student adds their names to a list. The money they are collecting, without telling me, will pay for Pablito's burial completely.

'Pablito, you are resting next to your grandmother Olga. Remember her words: "Right now, you are the small son of the great painter but soon you'll be the great son of the small painter." Your friends at the Cours Chateaubriand got the message. With their generous impulse, they testified to the fact that you were greater, infinitely greater, than Picasso the painter.'

The Protestant cemetery in Cannes. Among our friends from Cannes and Golfe-Juan, a man is hiding. He is crying. That man is my father. I have been too paralysed by grief to dare hope that he might come and ask his son for forgiveness.

— 13 —

I'm indifferent to everything. I get up, wash, roam around the house, walk past people and things without seeing them. I'm not even angry or indignant, I have no desire, no expectations. All I know is that Pablito is dead. Everything else is pointless.

Mienne — in my heart of hearts, I can no longer see her as my mother — talks about her distress non-stop.

'Your brother. Oh, your poor brother!' She weeps and moans, intoxicating herself on grief. 'I'm going to write a book. I'll record it all. Picasso and me . . . Picasso and your father . . . Picasso and your brother. Everything, I'll tell all.'

The Picasso virus has taken hold of her again. She gives interviews, stops people in the street. The grocer, the baker, the butcher, the chemist and all their customers become her captive audience.

'Oh, if only you knew my suffering!'

She talks about our poverty, the sacrifices she has had to make, her self-abnegation, the trials she endured, the insults she had to tolerate, while Picasso, the loathsome Picasso, was rolling in money.

'We had to beg for a morsel of bread.'

Everyone sympathizes with her sorrow. So much suffering merits compassion. This display of grief turns my stomach. I refuse to express my suffering. I say nothing and hide from the world. Locked in silence, I appear to be without feeling. A heartless creature who is ruthlessly rejected by her mother:

'There is no justice. You're the one who should have died.'

Me, and not Pablito. I'm a girl. I belong to the category of people for whom she has no love. To get her to love me, I submit to all her demands. I do the housework and make the meals, I do everything she asks. I waste away, become anorexic. She doesn't care. As far as she's concerned, I don't count.

I go back to my job at the hospice, back to my autistic and schizophrenic children. But now I can't bear their cries, their madness, their wretchedness. I have been too immersed in Pablito's wretchedness. I must get away and put a distance between my mother and me. I want to find myself, give myself a chance, and forget everything so I can finally be alone with the memory of my brother.

I quit my job and leave for London. There I find a student hostel where I can live for very little money. The hostel – the LTC school – takes in young women from all over Europe: girls from Germany, Italy, Spain and, of course, England. To distract myself, I go out in the evening with my friends. I attend football matches, explore the city, and take on small jobs to make money: as a baby sitter, a shop assistant in a record shop and then a clothes shop. On the days when I feel down, I phone my mother. In spite of all the harm she does me, I need to hear her voice. She either hangs up on me or tells me she doesn't have time to talk:

'Your timing is always bad.'

I will now skip over a whole part of my life.

It could have begun like a fairy tale with, 'Once upon a time' and ended with, 'They had lots of children.' When I was fifteen, my prince charming – because, of course, he had to be a prince – was a doctor. He was tall and had blue eyes. In my childish innocence, he had every possible virtue. A doctor relieves pain and I was in so much pain. I imagined that, one day, I would marry a man like him. Naive as I was, I idealized him and saw myself leaning my head on his shoulder. The man and his profession were connected in my mind.

Once upon . . .

Here I will leave a blank. A blank that I will only fill in for Gaël and Flore, the children I had with this man. This blank could be the subject of a whole book. But I'll never write it. However, I'm prepared to disclose its contents to Gaël and Flore one day, should they so desire. Though I've trained myself to be silent so as to remain alive, I promise to tell them the truth, the whole truth and nothing but the truth. In great detail. Then they will know the lengths I went to in order to give them the love they deserved, even if the price of that love was torment, pain and fear.

Gaël, I'd like you to know that you can be loved for being you. It is simple. Be yourself and don't try to cheat. The future is not a utopia. Bearing the name Picasso is hardly an accolade. Prefer the name Gaël. I was told that, in Irish, it means 'brave'. Be worthy of that name.

Flore, you will always amaze me. On horseback as in life, you jump over all obstacles – magnificently, brilliantly, and always with simplicity. A simplicity I love and of which I am so proud. If you want me to leaf through these blank pages with you one day, don't pull on the bit as you do with your horses. My mouth will find it so hard to confide all the things I endured when I was your age.

When, after eight months, I returned from London, I got in touch with my mother. I didn't want to live with her any more. The future father of my children had asked me to live with him. I had to try my luck. Come what may. I was only twenty-two years old.

My mother left my belongings on the doorstep of the Villa La Rémajo – not in a suitcase but in a dustbin bag.

I was an ungrateful daughter. I deserved nothing better than a grey dustbin bag.

Thursday, 5 June 1975. On the other end of the phone, I hear a voice that I don't recognize. It's Christine, my father's wife.

'Marina, your father has just died. He was very ill.' It's impossible for me to believe. It is just too dreadful. Grandfather dead, my brother dead, my father dead. No one is left and it makes me feel guilty – guilty that I'm still alive.

'When? Where? How?'

I would like to make up for the time and distance that separated me from my father. For him to live again through Christine's words.

'His last wish was to see Spain again . . . When he returned his state worsened . . . He didn't recover. He died last night.'

And, of course, the ritualistic phrase: 'He didn't suffer.'

He died two years after my brother. He was fifty-four years old.

On the analyst's couch, I asked my father's forgiveness so

many times, my father whom I never used to see. I asked him to forgive the harm his father had done him, to forgive my brother who had banished him from his memory, to forgive me for daring to pass judgement on him.

Who cared about the life he had?

No one. He wasn't famous.

A phone call from Claude, the son of Picasso and Françoise Gilot. Since 1974, he and his sister Paloma, together with Marie-Thérèse Walter's daughter, Maya Widmayer, have a legal right to the name Picasso and the title of heir.

'Marina, do you want to come to your father's funeral?'

'How can I? I don't have any money.'

'I'll send you your ticket.'

Claude comes to pick me up at Orly airport in Paris. I sense he's self-conscious and I'm self-conscious. We haven't seen each other in ages. He's surprised that I have no luggage. Only the blue jeans and clogs I'm wearing. I'm not trying to make a statement, it's just that, since my brother's death, I'm not even interested in buying the bare essentials.

'Tomorrow,' says Claude, 'you will see the lawyer in charge of your grandfather's estate. He will give you a cheque.'

A cheque? Why? I don't understand.

'In the meantime,' Claude adds, 'take this one-hundred-franc note. You can't go around Paris without any money on you.'

He takes me to his house on the Boulevard Saint-Germain. A luxurious apartment where his girlfriend and other people I don't know are waiting for us.

'Did you have a good trip? Do you want anything to drink? Do you want to be taken to your room now?'

They are so considerate and kind.

This may seem strange but when Claude asked me if I wanted to go to the hospital where my father's body was laid out, I said yes without a moment's hesitation. After so many years apart, I wanted to see him again. Maybe for the sake of Pablito, who had been turned away from Notre-Dame-de-Vie when grandfather died. I wanted to see him again – and make him exist.

My father was lying on a white bed. His face was contorted. I had the feeling he was suffering, even in death. I moved closer and put my hand on his crossed hands. Maybe I kissed him. Did I kiss him or simply touch him? Now I don't know, but in that dimly lit room, I wanted to make certain that it was really he – he who, alive, had been so absent and so weak. A cheek . . . a cold hand. That was all that was left.

The next day, Claude told me that he was taking me to his country house for the weekend.

'The funeral isn't until Tuesday. A refreshing break in the country will do you good.'

I have bad memories of that weekend in Normandy. First of all, because I didn't know anyone and felt left out, secondly because, being short of space, Claude had put me up in an isolated annexe all by myself where I spent the night trembling with fear. On Sunday night we returned to Paris. We had a dismal dinner at the Brasserie Lipp, in Saint-Germain-des-Près, where I couldn't follow the conversation. Then we went back to Claude's apartment.

'Good night, Marina. We wish Pablito had been with us tonight.'

It was the first time my brother had been mentioned. His suicide was disturbing. His death, indecent.

For the Spanish, funerals are a party, an opportunity to see relatives, cousins and friends that one hasn't seen in a long time. An *oportunidad* as they say over there. There's a dinner at which they all reminisce:

'Do you remember the day that . . .?'

People talk about Picasso – not about my father, but about the great Picasso.

'*Qué talento! Qué genio!*'

And they drink, eat and shout. *Abrazos*, laughter, full mouths, grins, knowing winks, a cacophony of voices. By tomorrow my father will be forgotten.

Among them is one of my grandfather's nephews. He comes up to me and whispers in my ear, 'It's good that you're alive.'

Paloma, Maya, Christine and her son Bernard, my half-brother, and all the others, gather around me.

'Marina, you must be brave.'

'Marina, you haven't had an easy life.'

'Marina, your grandfather, your brother and now your father. Poor little Marina.'

Poor little Marina. People are concerned about me. I exist in death.

The next day, I have an appointment with Maître Bacqué de Sariac, one of my grandfather's lawyers. He wants to give me an envelope that my father has left me. It contains a hundred thousand francs and a note in shaky handwriting:

'I'm leaving you this sum to help you. I hug you.' It is signed Paulo. Just Paulo.

'Your father wanted to give it to you himself,' Maître Bacqué de Sariac explains, 'but he didn't dare get in touch with you.'

I'd like to tell him that, in any case, I wouldn't have accepted this money from my father. I'd like to tell him . . . But what's the point? I have no resentment now. Just an envelope containing a hundred thousand francs. Repentance in the guise of a last allowance.

Claude goes to great lengths for me. I'm a provincial. He finds it normal to be steering me around the maze of the Paris business world.

'This afternoon, you'll be meeting Maître Zecri. He is expecting you. I phoned him.'

As a result of my father's death, my half-brother Bernard and I are now included in the Picasso estate in the same way as he, Jacqueline, Maya and his sister Paloma. He doesn't want trouble, he wants everything to go smoothly.

'You know, we've had our share of suffering too. We had a period of adversity too . . .' He wants to equalize our suffering, say we are all in the same boat, whereas I have lost Pablito . . .

I don't feel like replying. I don't owe anyone explanations, I have no scores to settle. I have only one thought: to extract myself from this business and escape from this family that is held together by interests from beyond the grave.

Maître Pierre Zecri, the lawyer in charge of the estate, receives me. My father hasn't made a will.

'Marina Picasso, daughter of Paul Picasso and Emilienne Lotte, his divorced wife, according to the statutes of intestate cases . . .'

I don't listen to him. I have other things on my mind. When I walked into his office, I broke the heel of one of my clogs and I have no other shoes to wear. My mind wanders. I don't feel concerned by all this legal talk. I'm pleased about one thing though: with the money contained in the envelope that my father left me and the cheque that Maître Zecri has given me as an advance, I will be able to reimburse Marie-Thérèse Walter, pay the last instalments on my VW and perhaps . . . Nothing. I have no desire for anything.

The first thing I do on my return to Golfe-Juan is deposit money in my mother's bank account, which is – of course – in the red. Oddly enough, my mother, who has always fantasized about the Picasso wealth, does not want to take advantage of the money that she could spend any way she wants. On the contrary, she continues to economize. Her delusions have switched gear. She is no longer haunted by my grandfather's power but by her own power:

'It's a good thing I'm here to administer my daughter's capital. It's a good thing she listens to me. She relies on me.'

The grocer, the baker, the butcher, the chemist and all their customers are full of admiration.

That's what's important to her.

14

When you have spent your childhood and adolescence begging for more love and a bit of attention, when you've never had a penny in your pocket and borne your name like a cross, when you've owned nothing and lost everything, to inherit is like being condemned. I know what some people will say: 'Her grandfather is famous, he leaves her a fortune, she has a lot of money . . . What is she complaining about?' I'm not complaining. I'm just trying to remember the facts as I lived them.

The first time I was invited to a discussion about the inheritance, I had no idea what was expected of me. I had only one desire – to escape the Picasso clan. In order to do so as quickly as possible, I turned down the share that my grandmother Olga had left to my father, and I turned down Pablito's share, which normally should have been divided between me and my half-brother Bernard. To be honest, I didn't want any complications. I was too badly wounded.

To be freer still, I had to buy up the usufruct rights of Christine; in other words, the portion of my inheritance that Christine, as my father's second wife, had an interest in during her lifetime. My own mother wasn't entitled to even so much as a penny. Very kindly − and because she knew what Pablito and I had endured − Christine accepted immediately. I was freed of the Picasso shackles.

The art expert Maurice Rheims had been given the task of valuing the thousands of works of art that were part of my grandfather's estate. Afterwards, he and a horde of lawyers went about dividing these works into as many lots as there were heirs. First of all, Jean Leymarie et Dominique Bozo − the directors of the Musée Picasso − selected the paintings, drawings, engravings and ceramics that the State had priority over by way of inheritance tax. Once we had settled the fees of Maître Rheims and the lawyers, Jacqueline, Maya, Paloma, Claude, Bernard and I could finally collect our inheritance. Of course, we first had to pay our individual inheritance taxes, which, in my case, came to the equivalent of half the wealth that my grandfather had left me.

I had not wanted to take part in these spoils. As I have said, it didn't interest me. When the director of the BNP bank in Paris offered to open the doors to the vault containing my share of Picasso's work, I flatly refused. I didn't feel strong enough to face this final stage. Since I hated the man for the suffering that my brother and I had endured, I found it illogical for me to own anything by him. I couldn't dissociate the artist from his work. I also inherited La Californie, with those gates that had kept us out, and its oppressive rooms that smelt of the forbidden. I didn't want it. I decided to sell it and buy back my soul.

I tried to get rid of it but I couldn't find a buyer, so in the end I kept it. I couldn't bear to live in it though: I found it too large and gloomy. I could hear the floors squeaking, the wind sweeping through the rooms. I was afraid of coming across Picasso's ghost.

The size of La Californie frightened me in the same way that, for a long time, everything did that I found particularly big. I remember the discomfort I felt, in the United States, when I was given Coca Cola in a glass that was too big, or an enormous container of popcorn. Coke, popcorn, huge avenues, wide-open spaces, skyscrapers, American cars, even the sky made me faint. In the course of my analysis, I came to realize that this phobia came from my grandfather. Because of the large place he occupied in my life.

Years later – Gaël and Flore had been born – I decided to look at my art collection. It was horrible. When I had the treasures in front of me, I was overcome by dizziness and had to leave the premises. Whenever I was asked to participate in an exhibition of my grandfather's work, I couldn't bring myself to go and, when I did, my anguish was so great that I would faint. On the advice of Jan Krugier – an art dealer, but more importantly, a friend to whom I had given the task of administering my collection – I had several paintings sent to the apartment in Cannes where I was living at the time. For months they remained turned against the wall in a room which I didn't dare enter because of the unbearable anguish they caused me.

I am often asked what this newly acquired wealth meant to me. What I did with it. In memory of my father, I bought a 125cc motorcycle, a Porshe and then, because he had dreamed of owning one, a Ferrari that I kept only for a short time. In memory of my grandmother Olga and her last days at the clinic where Pablito and I used to visit her,

I had a fur blanket made that revived her warmth and elegance. Finally, I gave all the friends from my childhood at Golfe-Juan refrigerators, coats, radios, televisions, cars … Probably because, at the time, we didn't have these things.

Afterwards, I bought a house at Cap d'Antibes, which I later gave to my mother. I certainly owed it to her.

I indulged myself. I certainly owed it to myself.

Finally, I was able to help children in distress halfway around the world – my Ho Chi Minh children. I certainly owed it to them.

Now money is a tool that gives me freedom, and that's all. I have a car I use to pick up my children at school, another car to take them on holiday and a jeep that I lend to Flore and her fiancé, Arnaud, who run a riding club in Valbonne. Though it may disappoint the people who think I live like a millionaire, I don't own a Mediterranean yacht and I have never rented a private plane for my trips; I don't stay in luxury hotels or go to trendy clubs where people go to be seen, or to tea rooms for ladies of leisure. I'm not a member of the jet set.

Out of decency, I've always refused child benefits and, so as not to profit from the free government health service, I've taken out private insurance for myself and my children. I can at least show that much propriety, that much respect.

But here again, I'll leave a blank.

I don't like talking about money. Perhaps because I have some. Or because I used not to have any when we lived in the shadow of a genius.

15

Picasso's genius.

The word 'genius', which experts on Picasso love to use, annoys me and makes me indignant. I can't understand how they can let themselves analyse his work in a redundant, pompous jargon aimed at a small group of initiates: 'The Hispanic mobility of the reds and browns', 'the cosmic impulse of the line', 'the composition's chimerical problematic'? How dare they presume to lock Picasso and his oeuvre inside a fortress whose key they alone possess?

Picasso and genius, genius and Picasso: two inseparable words that are useful for dinner parties.

'Picasso's terrific. Pure unadulterated genius! Please help yourself to some more asparagus. It comes from our property in Provence.'

And the comments overheard in bars:

'A genius. A genius. If I were Picasso, given the price of his paintings, I'd paint one and stop right there.'

The Picasso name — the name I bear — has become a trademark. It's in the windows of perfume and jewellery shops, on ashtrays, ties and T-shirts. You can't turn on the television without seeing a robot airbrushing the signature Picasso on the side of a car. Not to mention the Picasso Administration, the enterprise that manages the Picasso empire . . . which I have refused to be a part of.

Picasso, that forbidden grandfather whom I always saw wearing espadrilles, old shorts and a vest full of holes, that Spaniard who was much more of an Anarchist than a Communist, could never have imagined that – outside of his painting – his name would become a money-making machine.

After fourteen years of analysis, I've come to realize the extent to which the image I had of my grandfather was distorted. Through the prism of my father, he was contemptuous and stingy; through that of my mother, he was perverse and insensitive. Jacqueline, with her 'Monseigneur' dealt us the crowning blow: through her, we saw him as one of those cruel gods to whom the Aztecs offered human sacrifices.

Brought up on this myth, for a long time I held Picasso solely responsible for our misery. Everything was his fault: my father's failure, my mother's excesses, my grandmother Olga's decline, my brother Pablito's depression and death. I resented him for never thinking about our fate and for abandoning us. I couldn't understand why Pablito and I couldn't see him alone. I couldn't understand that he wasn't interested in his grandchildren when we demanded no more than a tiny drop of interest.

Now – and this is why I wanted to write this book – I realise that our grandfather was stolen from us. Pablito and I might have slipped casually into his life, but the irresponsibility of a father, a mother and a possessive wife stripped us of the affection that we craved for every time we visited him.

Surrounded by an atmosphere of such servility, how could this god have imagined that, behind each of our visits to La Californie, there was a cry for help?

Picasso would have had to descend for a moment from Mount Olympus and become, for the duration of a caress, a grandfather like any other ...

He couldn't. Isolated inside his work, he had lost all contact with reality and withdrawn into an impenetrable inner world.

This work was his only language, his only vision of the world. Even as a child, he had already entered an autistic universe. At school, in Malaga, while the other pupils listened to the teacher, he used to draw endless pictures of pigeons and bullfights in his exercise books. When his teachers reprimanded him, he would scoff at them. His drawings were as important as all the courses in arithmetic, Spanish and history.

He was insatiable and devoured life, people and things. A stone, a piece of wood or tile, a fragment of crockery, became creations in his hands. In the morning, he went jogging. He would tail the car, driven by Jacqueline. Along the way, he would throw on to the back seat a bit of scrap iron, a bicycle seat or some handlebars that he had found in the rubbish bins that lined his route. When he worked on them in his studio, the scrap iron, seat or handlebars were transformed into an owl, an African mask or a Minotaur.

For Picasso, the most banal object became a work of art.

The same was true of the women who had the privilege – or misfortune – of being swept up in his tornado. He submitted them to his animal sexuality, tamed them, bewitched them, ingested them, crushed them on to his canvas. After he had spent many nights extracting their essence, he would dispose of them, bled dry.

Like a vampire at dawn.

His magnetic gaze was like a scalpel; he would dig into reality, work on it, dismember it. Under his brush and hands, colours, clay, bronze, metal moulded themselves to his will. He subdued women and inert matter and made them his slaves.

Though his life spanned the century, he didn't live like his contemporaries. In fact, he didn't see them. His life was a sketchbook, a book of images roughed out by his dazzling creativity.

He didn't recreate the world; he imposed his own.

Throughout his life, in every period in his painting, he sought to track down the ephemeral and capture the moment. He wasn't painting, he wasn't drawing, he wasn't sculpting; he was pouring out everything he felt. He was dissecting his soul. Modesty and immodesty, vitality and death, violence and sensitivity, provocation and naivety, he made all those strings vibrate with such intensity that it electrified anyone who came near him.

And struck them down.

He was merciless in this quest for the absolute. Like Don Quixote he didn't care what weapon he used, he was compelled to fight and wreak revenge on a world that he wanted to master.

'A good painting,' he used to say, 'must be spiked with razor blades.'

This little man who was barely five foot three was *Yo Picasso*. Like the dazzling *matador* standing in the sandy arena, his only fear was death. His sword was a paintbrush; his *muleta* a virgin canvas.

Neither my father, my mother, Pablito nor I could understand the isolation in which this *matador* was struggling. No one had access to his bullfight – his eternal crusade. Who were we to think we could violate the arena in which he fought? What impudence to request of this man all the things that he had given up so he could dedicate himself to his art: money, family, tenderness, consideration. Those thousands of trivial things that are part of the everyday life of traditional families.

How could we reproach him for not understanding who we were, Pablito and I? Childhood, like everything else, could only be his creation.

'At eight, I was Raphaël,' he used to say. 'It took me a whole lifetime to paint like a child.'

We were his rivals.

The usual gamut of feelings had no hold at all over him. He liked money in order to buy houses in which he could paint. He would sell them as soon as they were too small to contain his new works. He didn't like to sit down at the table for a meal. This was time stolen from his creation. He had contempt for all the superficial things that money could buy. In his used clothes, he could have been mistaken for a tramp. He set no store by the court that crowded to see the master – his 'frog pond', as he called it.

By the end of his life, he had turned everyone away so he could be alone and use his last remaining strength to create.

We were among those he had turned away.

Thanks to analysis, I've been able to discover a grandfather that I didn't know. I used to wait for him to open the gate behind which he had taken refuge. Perhaps he wanted to open it. I'll never know. Perhaps, by the time he wanted to open the gate, it was too heavy and he was too tired.

In the end, who was more egotistical, Picasso or me?

Isolated inside Notre–Dame–de–Vie, he died in the same way as he had lived: alone, which is how he had wanted to be.

He had made this cruel statement: 'When I die, it will be a shipwreck. When a large ship goes down, many people in the vicinity are swept into the whirlpool.'

Many were indeed swept into the whirlpool.

Pablito, my inseparable brother, committed suicide two days after our grandfather was buried at Vauvenargues.

My father, the weak giant, died two years later feeling desperately orphaned.

Marie–Thérèse Walter, the inconsolable muse, hanged herself from the ceiling of her garage in Juan–les–Pins.

Jacqueline, the companion of his last days, also committed suicide with a bullet in her temple.

Later, Dora Maar died in poverty surrounded by the Picasso paintings she had refused to sell, so she could preserve for herself the presence of the man whom she idolized.

I was meant to be one of those victims. If I'm still around, I owe it to a lust for life and for struggle that I inherited from a grandfather I dreamed about . . .

And who wasn't there.

— 16 —

I have put down my bag, like a sailor who has been sailing the seven seas for a lifetime. I don't want it weighing on my shoulder any more. It's much too heavy — too heavy and too shabby.

Sitting — not lying — in my analyst's office, I finally take my fate into my own hands.

I am Marina Picasso.

'That's good,' the analyst says simply.

He understands that I am ready to turn a page.

As my analysis helped me towards the light, the most important thing in my life became my children, Gaël and Flore. I had been unable to devote myself to them completely during my 'dark years'. I wanted to find them again, get to know them, help them to get to know me. Gently, step by step. Like a convalescent . . .

China, Africa, Russia . . . Together we discovered the world; the sights made a striking impression on us and brought us closer together. The happiness my children felt, and the happiness they gave me, sharpened my maternal feelings. As I gradually rediscovered the world, I felt a desire to have more children. Gaël, who was now seven, and Flore, who was eight, liked the idea. They too wanted brothers and sisters.

'What about adopting children?' they asked me.

'I'd like to – if you agree.'

'Yes, we agree!'

We sealed a pact.

Monique, the guide at the Kuoni agency who organized every one of our trips, came to dinner with a Vietnamese friend. Her friend, François, had been educated in France but had always maintained close ties with his country. Encouraged by his kindness and his passion when he talked about Vietnam, I told him about my plan to adopt. He listened to me and – after what might have been construed as a cross-examination – said that he thought I would have no difficulty in adopting a Vietnamese child.

'There are so many children seeking a family. There are so many who are dying . . .'

He knew a doctor who worked at the Grall children's hospital in Ho Chi Minh City, the former French Military Hospital of Saigon. He would talk to her about me.

'Who is she?'

'Madame Hoa has used part of her wealth to help the underprivileged children of Ho Chi Minh City. She was Minister of Health for many years. Today she works in research and tries to improve the living conditions of the girls and boys under her care in the hospital.'

'When can I see her?'

'I'm leaving in a few days. As soon as I return, I'll get in touch with you.'

All I had to do was wait.

When François told Madame Hoa of my request, she quickly made all the necessary arrangements to help me. She found a baby for me. Like François, Madame Hoa had been educated in Paris. As fate would have it – coincidence or destiny? – she had known my grandfather in the nineteen fifties. They had belonged to the same Communist Party cell in the eighteenth *arrondissement* of Paris.

Ho Chi Minh City and its airport. The hassle of the customs. Gaël and Flore's excitement. My own impatience. Soon, I'll be holding in my arms the child I want so badly, the child of my resurrection.

His name will be Florian.

As we ride in the minibus that has come to pick us up, we discover the streets, the picturesque houses, the artisans' stalls, the bustling crowd, the colours, the fragrance, the smells – of spice, of musk, of mugginess.

The smells of paradise . . .

At the far end of the city, a baby is waiting for us.

But when we arrive, the Grall Hospital nursery has just locked its doors. We'll have to come back in the morning to meet Florian. I'm disappointed. A night can be endless when you've lived off hopes for so long and off a trust that is usually disappointed.

Florian is here, scrawny and tiny. Doctor Hoa had arranged for him to come from the Go Vap orphanage so she could care for him before entrusting him to me. His limbs are emaciated. Like all children who have suffered mal-nutrition, his stomach is bloated. He is only three months old, but he has lively look in his eyes.

'Picasso's eyes,' Madame Hoa says to me in a whisper.

I smile. Picasso's eyes – a legacy that fills me with joy.

I still have a few days left before returning to France with Florian in my arms. In the meantime, Madame Hoa offers to take me to visit the orphanages and hospitals that she's in charge of. She tells me that in Ho Chi Minh City alone, it is estimated that twenty-one thousand children have been abandoned and have to fend for themselves on the streets. Only fifteen hundred were counted in the census.

I see wretched orphanages, hospitals and hospices where children, elderly people and sick people are crowded together. Because of poverty and a lack of funds, the hygiene is dreadful. My heart bleeds. I must do something and I have so little time.

I contact the People's Committee, the Communist Party leaders, the Social Services. I move heaven and earth. This country has given me a child; I should help it.

My name pleads in my favour. As the granddaughter of Comrade Picasso, the people I contact listen to me and encourage me. They agree to take part in my humanitarian action.

'To cook a bowl of rice, the heat must marry the grains' – a Vietnamese proverb.

The head of the Social Services, in charge of health problems in the south of the country, offers to show me land in Thu Doc, in the northern suburbs of Ho Chi Minh City. He knows that I want to build a village for unfortunate children. I don't yet know how I'll go about it, but I want my wealth to serve a purpose. I'm not Mother Theresa but the suffering of the orphans that I witnessed in the institutions I visited with Madame Hoa was intolerable to me. I must throw myself into this completely and do everything possible for them.

Thu Doc is a former military area five thousand metres square, covered with marshes, water holes caused by the monsoon, and subtropical, chaotic vegetation: mangrove swamps, bamboo groves, palm trees run wild. On the edge of the land, there is a dilapidated building with peeling walls stained with saltpeter.

At my request, the head of the Social Services takes me around. Outside, there are orphans playing ball like children everywhere in the world. Inside, all alone in a large room, a small boy in striped pyjamas looks at me. He's balding, his face is emaciated and his eyes are sad and poignant. He knows he will die of the cancer that is devastating him. He's only eight years old.

The decision is made: with the agreement of the Vietnamese authorities, Thu Duc will become 'The Village of Youth'.

If this village exists today, it is thanks to Florian, to the little boy in striped pyjamas, and especially to my brother Pablito. The three hundred and fifty children who can live a dignified life there owe it to them.

Memories and the expressions in eyes can perform miracles.

On the return flight, I hold Florian close against me. He is tightly grasping Gaël's index finger in his right hand and Flore's little finger in his left.

Through the windows, we see the sky spotted with clouds.

Cannes and La Californie, where the doors are wide open to welcome Florian. La Californie, where laughter rings out in every room and children can live a childhood that should have been mine and Pablito's – a childhood full of concern, care and attentiveness.

'What time does baby wake up?'

'When are you giving baby his bath?'

'Did you remember baby's bottle?'

The word 'baby' that Gaël and Flore are bubbling over with as they look down into Florian's crib invigorates and stimulates me. More babies are waiting for me in Vietnam. I must act fast.

Between two visits to Lenval Hospital to have Florian examined, I see the architect who renovated La Californie for me. I hand him the plans that the Vietnamese authorities have given me so that he can draw up the plans for the Village of Youth in collaboration with an architect from Ho Chi Minh City. I don't want buildings resembling barracks for Thu Duc; I want him to build little houses that will each have a kitchen, a bathroom, a dining room and bedrooms. I also want a school, a gymnasium, a sports stadium, a swimming pool, a park. I want . . . I want . . . I want the children who will live there to find a family. The love they didn't have.

That's the least that life owes them.

I return to Vietnam. Once again, Gaël and Flore are there to help me. We have agreed among us to adopt other little children – if I were to listen to them, *many* little children. 'Babies', as they say.

At Ho Chi Minh City airport, a red carpet has been spread out at the foot of the gangway and, under the red flag with a yellow star, the highest dignitaries of the country are waiting for me. It is not me that they have come to honour but my grandfather, the father of the Dove and of Guernica.

'Comrade Picasso, did you have a good trip?'

'Comrade Picasso, this country is yours.'

I am a native child of this land.

While the architects and their workers begin work at the construction site that will become, six months later, the first segment of the Village of Youth, I visit Madame Hoa at Grall Hospital where May, a little one-and-a-half-year-old girl, is waiting for me. Just like Florian, May comes from the Go Vap orphanage. Like him, She is seriously malnourished. The only people she's familiar with are the nurses and staff at Go Vap and Grall Hospital. She won't let me near her; she refuses to come out of her cocoon. She struggles and screams. I must be careful not to rush her. I know it will be difficult to cut her roots, roots that, since birth, have been nourished on misfortune. The only sap she knows.

My life is divided between Vietnam and Europe. In 1990 the Village of Youth is complete, but I still want to develop its reception facilities and buy the neighbouring military land. Construction starts again with the same energy, the same faith. Meanwhile, my Foundation arranges for regular shipments of several tons of milk to the orphanages and hospitals of Ho Chi Minh City, and organizes the digging of artesian wells in inland villages. It grants a subsidy to a village of retired people and veterans so that they can raise livestock and begin farming, and it gives scholarship help to two hundred students at the University of Daklat, in the north-east of Ho Chi Minh City. Because of the poor state of the children's hospitals and their inadequate medical equipment, my Foundation, with subsidies from France, supports the renovation of two paediatric hospitals in the Capital and finances the creation of surgical and intensive care units. Furthermore I decide to pay tribute to Madame Hoa by modernizing the Go Vap orphanage which was a home to Florian and May. With the consent of the authorities, improvements are made inside; it is repainted and given new furniture. Seamstresses are hired to make clothes for the children. Covered playgrounds are built so they can play during the rainy season.

I follow my instincts, do what I feel I must do. I don't calculate. I deal with the most urgent matters first.

As Picasso used to say, I don't seek, I find.

Another trip to Ho Chi Minh City with Gaël, Flore and May, who is two and a half years old. Florian, who is twenty months, has stayed in France. We have come to pick up Dimitri in an orphanage run by the charity Terre des Hommes.

As soon as I saw fifteen-month-old Dimitri, I knew that he was the one – the new child who would join our family. Abandoned when he was only three days old, Dimitri knew nothing of the world. Every little thing seemed to fascinate him: a bird flying past the window, a gust of wind blowing through a tree, the sound of a faraway car. Finger pointing up, he marvelled at these minor miracles, and his exclamations of wonder, his 'Oh!'s were such tender music to my ears that I knew I had to adopt him. We had him examined at the Carpentier Foundation in Saigon and then took him home with great pomp. He had not yet learned to walk; he preferred to hang on to me, like a drowning person hangs on to a life jacket. 'Your arms . . . your arms' were the only words with which he rewarded me for many months to come. Arms that were wide open for him.

That's my life. Invited to its banquet, I have done what I can and what I thought I had to do. Sometimes good, sometimes bad.

'When I don't have any blue, I use red,' my grandfather used to say.

I have had to use the colours offered to me by fate. Some were primary, others complementary. Tints and half-tints. I hope my children will not pass judgement on the work that was my life when they hang it on the wall of their memory.

Gaël has phoned me from London. He is expecting me next week.

Flore and Arnaud are stopping by to see me tomorrow after having cared for their horses at the Mougins riding school.

Florian, now eleven and a half, is at his judo class. This morning he told me about his plans for the future. He is going to be a cook and, if that doesn't work out, head of a platoon in the national police force.

May, who is twelve, wants be a French teacher or a film star.

Dimitri, who is ten, wants be an airline pilot, but also an architect – on the days when Air France is on strike.

It's five in the evening. The sun is setting over the Iles de Lérins.

I'm at peace with myself.